Barbara Aiello

Aging Jewishly

What Our Traditions Tell Us About Growing Old

Hakodesh Press

Imprint

Any brand names and product names mentioned in this book are subject to trademark, brand or patent protection and are trademarks or registered trademarks of their respective holders. The use of brand names, product names, common names, trade names, product descriptions etc. even without a particular marking in this work is in no way to be construed to mean that such names may be regarded as unrestricted in respect of trademark and brand protection legislation and could thus be used by anyone.

Cover image: www.ingimage.com

Publisher:
Hakodesh Press
is a trademark of
International Book Market Service Ltd., member of OmniScriptum Publishing Group
17 Meldrum Street, Beau Bassin 71504, Mauritius
Printed at: see last page
ISBN: 978-620-2-45505-3

For Carolyn Kaplan

My Mentor and Friend

whose life of selfless dedication

to preserving and honoring

our Jewish traditions

inspires me every day

Table of Contents

Introduction

"With age comes wisdom, and length of days brings understanding." The Book of Job, 12:12

These words, profound in their simplicity, were uttered by a biblical figure that might have had other more pressing issues on his mind. The words come from Job, our "poster child" for heartache, pain and suffering.

In fact in the midst of his trials when Job's so called "friends" stop by to offer constructive criticism regarding the tragedies that have defined Job's life, Job takes time to clarify his position. He emphasizes that wisdom does not come from years of study or the practice of philosophical debate or even the need to sound smart. Job believes that wisdom is grounded in humility and the wise person is one who is simply seeking and trusting that living an ethical life guarantees the wisdom of the ages.

In 2009 I began a Jewish journey that led me to not only serve as rabbi to men and women in a (Sarasota, FL) Jewish retirement community but to live among the residents as well. I viewed my apartment in the Independent Living wing of what then was called Kobernick House as a stroke of convenience – not having to drive to work or even cook dinner - as my job description included eating my evening meal alongside residents in the community dining room.

What I didn't understand at first, but what I came to cherish as the greatest benefit of all, was the opportunity to live among the residents, to share in their daily joys, sorrows, ups and downs.

With my residents I rode the bus to local events, danced at the New Year's Eve gathering and met their friends and families in our beautiful common area, The Rotunda."

As their rabbi, I adapted Jewish rituals, synagogue services, festivals and holidays to meet the needs of our most fragile. As their spiritual guide I visited them in the hospital and held their hands as they passed to "HaOlam HaBa" the world to come.

From all of these experiences – punctuated with sadness and joy, "tusris" and "simcha," irony, sarcasm and great good humor, this book was born.

The selections were chosen from among my guest columns for the Sarasota/Manatee (Florida) Jewish News. Readers wrote to encourage me to collect these stories so that families, residents and staff in the nearly 200 Jewish care facilities in North America could share what biblical Job would term the humble wisdom of the ages.

This book, "Aging Jewishly" is a tribute and a thank you to all of the elderly men and women who shared the wisdom of their life experiences with me in my ten years as their resident rabbi. Thanks to each resident whom I had the honor of knowing, It is thanks to them that I am a more modest, compassionate and humble rabbi than I could have ever hoped to be.

HOW TO USE THIS BOOK

This collection of Jewish themed and generally themed stories, based on the experiences of elderly Jewish men and women and supplemented with supportive research and statistics, offers not only the individual reader but Activities, Program and Spiritual Life staff of Jewish (and secular) care facilities as well as synagogues, churches, support groups and senior organizations the opportunity to approach difficult topics with elderly residents in either one on one meetings or in small group discussion.

The book's structure allows for program staff to create a series of group meetings or presentations surrounding a central theme, such as **Ritual and Tradition, Relationships, Risibility and Resilience issues including Caring, Coping and Moving Forward.**

Discussion questions at the end of each section, **"Gleanings and Meanings,"** offer the reader/listener an opportunity to explore some of the articles' themes that on a personal basis, might otherwise be difficult to discuss. Note that issues such as "Divorced Aging Parents," "Elderly Isolation," "Seniors and Sex," just to name a few, are appropriate for any of our elders, regardless of ethnic or religious background.

PART I:

Rituals and Traditions

"Judaism teaches us to be attached to holiness in time."
Abraham Joshua Heschel

Hava Nagila – Ten Fabulous Facts for Bubbys and Zaydes to Share

1. **Hava Nagila, a melody that originated more than 200 years ago, was born as a song without words** (in Hebrew, "niggun"). During the era of forced inscription into the Czarist Russian army, young Jewish boys were taken from their families to serve 25 years as soldiers for the Czar. It was during this time of great sadness that Rabbi Yisroel Friedman encouraged Jews to find joy and purpose in life. Hava Nagila's melody and the humming of this wordless tune became a song of hope for many shtetl Jews.

2. **Hava Nagila made its way from Europe to Jerusalem**. At the turn of the last century Chassidim from Austria brought Rabbi Friedman's melody to Jerusalem. In about 1915 these Chassidic Jews met with a musical pioneer who gifted Hava Nagila with its memorable lyrics.

3. A native Latvian, passionate Zionist, and world renowned musicologist, **Abraham Zvi Idelson, wrote the words to Hava Nagila**.

4. **Hava Nagila's lyrics are based on the words from Psalm 11 verse 24**: *Ze ha'yom asah Adonai, nagila v'nismecha*

bo, "This is the day the Lord has made, rejoice and be happy in it."

5. Some are unsure of the lyrics. **Refresh your memory with the words to Hava Nagila.**

Hava nagila, Hava nagila = Let's rejoice, Let's rejoice

Hava nagila v'nismecha = Let us rejoice and be glad

Hava neranana, Hava neranana = Let's sing, let's sing

Hava neranena v'nismecha = Let's sing and be glad

Uru, uru achim = Awake, awake brothers

Uru achim b'lev sameach = Awake brothers with a joyful heart.

6. **At the formal conclusion of World War I**, Idelson organized a celebratory concert in Jerusalem. The chorus sang Hava Nagila and **it became an instant hit, first in Jerusalem and then throughout the Jewish world.**

7. **Hava Nagila made its way from the kibbutz to Jewish Zionist camps, many in America.** Jewish children took the song home and sang it at their Bar and Bat Mitzvah celebrations and later on at their weddings, with the guests of honor carried high on chairs.

8. **In the 1950's Hava Nagila became part of the mainstream music scene** thanks to Harry Belafonte who closed his concerts with the uplifting melody. "I was always moved by this song," Belafonte said. Could be because, according to the *Dictionary of Sephardic (Jewish) surnames*, Belafonte is a Spanish Jewish name!

9. **More and more international stars added Hava Nagila to their repertoire**, from Connie Francis to Glenn Campbell to Europe's "Barbra Streisand", Dalida' (who said "This melody is in my blood.") to Olympic gold medalist Ally Raisman who performed her winning gymnastic routine to Hava Nagila's internationally recognized beat.

10. **PBS produced a film, "Hava Nagila The Movie," and YouTube boasts more than one half million videos featuring Hava Nagila**, a song that, in the words of Dr. Yvette Alt Miller, "convey(s) a deeply felt Jewish truth: that we all long to transcend the challenges in our lives… that all of us want to be happy. And that singing and listening to the happiness in Hava Nagila can bring us all a measure of joy."

Thanks to journalists Dr. Yvette Alt Miller (Aish.com) and Dr. James Loeffler (My Jewish Learning) for their research on this topic.

Gleanings and Meanings:

1. What fact about Hava Nagila did you find most fascinating?

2. Do you recall a time when you danced the Hora with Hava Neglia as the dance melody? What was the event and why do you remember it so well?

3. In your opinion why is Hava Negila still so popular today?

"Where's My Ketubah?"

"Can you believe it?" Fritizi said, shaking her head at her mahjong buddies. "My granddaughter is getting married to a nice Catholic boy so I was so surprised when she wanted to see my ketubah – from 71 years ago. Of course I'm "kvelling", but first I have to find it!"

Fritzi's ketubah, (the Hebrew word for the Jewish wedding document) was standard fare generations ago when two Jews married under the chuppah in a Jewish ceremony. Back then the Jewish Interfaith marriage rate was in single digits and interfaith couples who wished to marry under the chuppah were often denied a Jewish ceremony. These weddings often took place in City Hall where the union was formalized legally and where the Jewish marriage document, the ketubah, was non-existent.

How times have changed. Today the interfaith marriage rate among one Jewish partner and a partner of a different religion lies somewhere between 47 and 70 percent and many interfaith couples include an interfaith ketubah in their wedding ceremony as a way to publicly acknowledge their respect for both faith traditions and their pledge to create a loving home where these traditions are encouraged, observed and respected.

A "ketubah" (pronounced "ka-too-bah") is the name given to the Jewish wedding document which historians believe has been in use for millennia. The word *ketubah* derives from the Hebrew verb "to write," and its history dates back to the Book of Genesis where Abraham's servant asked Rebecca if she would consent to marry Isaac. Rebecca said, "Yes," and the rest is Biblical history!

To seal the agreement we read that (Abraham's family) "brought forth jewels of silver, and jewels of gold, and raiment, and gave them to Rebecca." – an example of the first marriage contract. Later, traditional Judaism introduced the ketubah, a binding legal document that enumerates all of the requirements that a husband is obliged to fulfill to his wife.

Researchers agree that the ketubah tradition dates back 2000 years with the discovery of what is thought to be the earliest ketubah – found in Egypt and written on papyrus. The year was about 440 B.C.E making this ketubah one of the earliest documented examples of the granting of legal and financial rights to women.

It was in Italy where the traditional ketubah underwent its first major change – the adding of decorative art to the document. The first embellished ketubah was written in the Jewish settlement of Ancona where this artistic tradition was born and soon most ketubot were adorned with bright colors and gold leaf accents. Italian ketubah artists traditionally created a wide margin around the Hebrew text to give themselves room to depict Biblical scenes, drawings of Jewish ritual items and even zodiac signs. Examples of these elaborate and intricate ketubot are on display in the Jewish museum of Rome.

Recent years has brought another adaptation – the writing of egalitarian, same sex and interfaith ketubot, with couples choosing to incorporate wording that expresses their own unique relationship – a relationship that Bubby Fritzi explained to her friends at the mahjong table. She says, "So, nu, my granddaughter told me all about the ketubah they are designing and she wants the artist to see my ketubah and use some of the words to tie our generations together!"

When Fritzi's granddaughter and her fiancé sign their interfaith ketubah they will continue an ancient tradition that connects them, l'dor v'dor, from generation to generation, all the way back to the Jews of ancient times. Their ketubah represents the promises made on their wedding day and the promises that they will keep throughout their lives.

For Fritzi and her family the revival of an ancient tradition and the widening of the traditional circle to include interfaith couples represent a golden opportunity. Like Fritizi we can applaud our grandchildren's respect for Jewish traditions and open our hearts to support the new family created through the signing of the ancient document – the ketubah.

Gleanings and Meanings:

1. Do you have your ketubah? If so, where is kept? What meaning does it have for you?

2. Do you remember your wedding ceremony and/or a wedding ceremony that you attended? What are your favorite elements of a Jewish wedding?

3. Years ago most rabbis would not officiate at an interfaith wedding? Did that happen to you or to anyone you know? If so, how was the situation resolved? How did it make the couple feel?

Let's "Dish" About the Seder Plate!

"It goes back a long time," said Dora as she hugged the cream-colored china plate to her chest. "My grandmother used it and so did my mother and now it's mine." Dora was reminiscing about her family's seder plate, the literal centerpiece of her family's Passover table.

These days seder plates come in all sorts of shapes, sizes, colors and designs and these mainstay items of Jewish tradition have a rich history all their own.

In ancient times our sages taught that in anticipation of the Passover holiday, we Jews should prepare a specially made, large wicker container in which to place Passover's symbolic foods. This wicker container would then be displayed on the seder table.

That's right. The first seder plate wasn't made of china or ceramic, pewter or silver – it was more like a wicker basket. And it most likely wasn't round. In fact historians tell us that the actual name was "*ke'arah*" which is the Hebrew word, not for "plate" but for "tray."

We find the first mention of what was to become the central focus of the seder table, the plate or the "*ke'arah*," in the Mishnah. Written in about the third century C. E., the Mishnah, which is the earliest compilation of Jewish Oral Law, features most of the rituals and prayers required for the Passover seder including directions for preparing what has become known as the seder plate.

Later, during the medieval period when Ashkenazi Jews began to write and publish *"haggadot,"* (the booklet used at the Passover seder to explain the meaning of the Exodus from Egypt), drawings of a large, round seder plate began to appear in the illustrations. However, the haggadot published by the Sephardi Jews of Spain, Portugal, Italy, as well as in the Middle East, often depicted the seder plate as the traditional wicker basket.

But before long Sephardic Jewish communities, whose artisans had learned to create ceramic art, moved away from the wicker basket and in 15th century Spain began to craft large ceramic plates replete with illustrations highlighting not only Jewish but Islamic culture as well. Thus the Passover seder plate e as an art form was born.

In 18th-century Germany, Jews who were asked to make seder plates made of pewter began to add engraved illustrations, Hebrew phrases and inscriptions to the plates themselves, while wealthy families in 18th and 19th century Germany commissioned ornate silver plates that featured intricately engraved scenes from the haggadah. Later on Jewish artisans were commissioned to create a three-tiered seder plate with a special opening designed to contain the three pieces of matzah, the unleavened bread that was carried by Jewish women during our escape from slavery in Egypt.

Today seder plates are often passed down in families, from grandparents, to parents to children, and in some cultures the plate itself makes a grand entrance to the seder table.

In Morocco the seder plate is brought to the Passover table with great ceremony. Covered with a beautiful transparent cloth, the plate is carried by the seder leader as the assembled guests greet its arrival with a joyful song.

In Tunisia, Southern Italy and the islands of Sicily and Sardinia the seder plate is also welcomed with great aplomb as it is carried to the table by the "lady of the house." It is customary that she then holds the plate over the head of the seder leader who then takes the plate and standing behind each guest, holds the plate over each person's head. The seder begins in this manner to demonstrate that although we were once slaves in Egypt and carried heavy burdens on our heads, today we are free to choose to "carry" the seder plate, a symbol of the precious gift of freedom.

Gleanings and Meanings:

1. Do you have a seder plate? Do you remember the seder plate from your childhood? What did these plates look like?

2. Did your family enjoy a Passover seder? What are your fondest seder memories?

3. Is a ritual items like a seder plate important to Jewish families? Why or why not?

The "Off-Night" Secret Seder - "Seder Hamishi"

"We'd better call the kids," said Al, cell phone in hand and poised to dial. "It's nearly Passover so we've got to organize the seder!" Al's wife Debra agreed and in seconds, thanks to the internet phenomenon, Zoom, they were talking simultaneously to their four grown children and six grandchildren, all whom are scattered from Seattle to Montreal.

But smiles turned to frowns when the family checked the calendar to find that the first and second night Seders would fall on a Wednesday and Thursday night. "Bummer," was all grandson Alex could say and everyone agreed. Work, school and sports schedules made it impossible for Al and Deb's family to share this Pesach holiday together. The alternative? The Sephardic style Hamishi Secret Seder.

Some historians believe that the Russian painter, Moshe Maimon's most famous work, "Marranos: Secret Seder," actually tells the story of the Seder Hamishi, a special Passover seder, held, not on the first or second night of Passover, but, as its name suggests, on the fifth night of the holiday.

Legend has it that during the time of the Inquisition, first in Spain, then in Portugal and finally on the islands of Sicily and

Sardinia and into Italy's mainland, Jews who had been forced into Christian conversion (*b'nei anusim* as they are called) were offered help, surprisingly, by their Christian neighbors.

"*Neofiti,*" as these persecuted Jews but now newly minted Christians were called, continued to arouse the suspicion of Inquisition authorities – so much so that gardeners, maids, cooks and nannies who worked in households of converted Jews were offered a bounty if they could catch their employers cleaning the house of "*chametz,*" (leavened bread), changing pots, pans and dishes, or preparing "*pane azimo,*" or "*matzah,*" the unleavened bread eaten during the Passover holiday.

And then, when the first night of Passover finally arrived, Inquisition soldiers, who laid in wait for the sun to set, would burst through the doors of what had once been Jewish homes, checking to see if any of these former Jews were "judaizing," - in this case, making Passover in secret.

Observing this injustice, some courageous Christians concocted a plan to help their Jewish neighbors. At great personal peril to themselves and their families (Christians who helped Jews were often tortured and murdered along with the Jews they tried to save), these Christians encouraged their Jewish neighbors to hold a seder, not on the first or second night, but, in order not to arouse the authorities' suspicions, at an alternative time, often on the fifth night.

Stories are told of Christian families who allowed Jews to sneak into their Christian "*cantinas*," (basement rooms) and under the cover of darkness, these Jewish neighbors first made the space kosher and then actually observed Passover complete with symbolic foods, prayers and blessings.

Over the years the fifth night seder became known as the Seder Hamishi – a doubly appropriate name especially since "hamish" is the Yiddish word for cozy, homey and friendly.

As rabbi of an Italian b'nei anusim community, I have initiated the Hamishi Secret Seder designed to bring our synagogue members together with local Christian families to tell the story and share Sephardic Passover traditions.

Symbolic seder foods include the traditional shank bone, but for us anusim it is coupled with the "bietola," (blood red beet) to symbolize the lamb's blood on the doorposts that saved the firstborn in Hebrew families. Locally grown romaine lettuce (more bitter than the American variety) replaces horseradish and pieces of celery stalk, rather than parsley, serve as "karpas," the green vegetable that is dipped in vinegar, rather than salt water.

The seder meal begins with a "primo piatto" of rice steamed with vegetables, because in our Sephardic or Mediterranean tradition, rice as well as other *kitniyot* are considered kosher for Pesach. Roasted lamb is a must along with *"mina,"* a layered lasagna-type meat, spinach and matzah pie brought to Italy from Spain by our crypto-Jewish ancestors.

Pesach anusim traditions begin with the lighting of the memorial candle in honor of our "forced ones," followed by the candle blessing for *Yom Tov,* sung in an ancient Ladino melody. The seder plate itself is actually a "ke'arah," a woven basket-type tray covered with silk netting that makes a grand entrance to the seder table after the kindling of light.

At the chanting of *"Ha lachma anya,"* the plate of matzah is passed shoulder to shoulder among the guests, a symbol of the heavy burden of slavery. The singing of *Dayenu* features green onion stalks that guests use to tap each other, symbolizing the sound of the whips used to beat the Hebrew slaves, while the recitation of the Ten Plagues includes placing the ten droplets of red wine in an old tin can which is later carried outdoors, symbolizing our wish that evil will stay far from our door.

For Al and Debra, they can consider making a seder on the third, fourth or fifth night of Pesach which often falls during the weekend – a more convenient time for families who live long distances to gather. As they come together, families have the unique opportunity to celebrate our Jewish brothers and sisters - Jews who were nearly robbed of their religion, culture and heritage and our nameless Christian protectors whose courage helped preserve the very traditions that we Jews are able to enjoy today.

NOTE: For a detailed description of Hamishi Passover traditions and recipes see "Too Good to Passover, Sephardic and Judeo-Arabic Seder Menus and Memories from Africa, Asia and Europe," Jennifer Felicia Abadi (pp. 590 - 625)

Gleanings and Meanings:

1. Sephardic Passover traditions differ from Ashkenazi traditions. What Sephardic tradition did you find most interesting and/or unusual?

2. Why is the meaning behind the creation of the Hamishi Seder an important element to celebrate?

3. Do you know anyone whose Jewish ancestry includes the crypto-Jewish, maranos or conversos experience? Why is it important to recognize and welcome these individuals?

4. Would you consider making a Hamishi Seder for your family? Why or why not?

Rededicate Your Home on Chanukah

Polly said, "It's early this year," and Helen agreed. Edith confessed that she just wasn't ready, while George complained that his retirement community prohibited the use of lighted candles, "So how am I gonna make Chanukah this year?" Joyce said it all with a sigh and an "Oi!"

Regardless whether you consider it a blessing that Chanukah comes early in December – "I like it early" says Karin, "because it doesn't compete with Christmas," - or later in the month as Sam prefers because, "When Chanukah comes later, then my grandkids are off from school and we can celebrate together," – there are creative ways to celebrate Chanukah and one of the most interesting is to inaugurate a *"Chanukah HaBayit"* or a rededication of your home.

The ceremony has historical roots. After the Maccabees' victory against the army of King Antiochus, the Jews reclaimed the Temple by performing a ceremony to restore it as a sacred and holy place.

The ceremony was called *"Chanukat HaBayit,"* which is a Hebrew phrase that meant "rededicating the house." Our sages tell us that our ancestors kindled special oil lamps and in the glow of the menorah light, we Jews reclaimed our home.

Today Chanukah can be a special time to remember that our homes are our sanctuaries and that each of the eight nights of Chanukah can offer our families an opportunity to rededicate our homes to our Jewish traditions. Each night, as we kindle our candles, or twist a bulb on our electric *chanukiyah*, we can renew the light of the spirit within each room.

Thanks to CLAL's National Jewish Resource Center, a new ritual of rededication can add depth and meaning to the Chanukah experience.

On each of the eight nights, before kindling the Chanukah lights, begin with a meditation:

"My home is the place where I celebrate life, mark the seasons, welcome guests, light candles, remember the past, dream about the future, and open my heart to the present. At Chanukah, may I rededicate my home to the values and relationships I hold sacred."

Then make this special blessing each night before kindling the candles:

"As this menorah fills with light, may our home be rededicated to the Source of Blessing that connects us all."

Eight Ways to Dedicate Your Home:

The First Candle: Invite guests, cook a special meal together, plan a family event or make time for those you love, creating and expanding "*shalom bayit*," relationships of peace.

The Second Candle: Revitalize your home as a center for Jewish learning. Add a new book to your Jewish book shelf.

The Third Candle: Invite a friend and together read a chapter from your new Jewish book. Share your thoughts and opinions. "Talk among yourselves!"

The Fourth Candle: Choose a place in your home where you can devote yourself to prayer, meditation or reflection. CLAL suggests making a "*mizrach*," a marker pointing eastward, and placing it on your own eastern wall to focus your attention toward Jerusalem.

The Fifth Candle: In solidarity with our brothers and sisters in Israel, use your *mizrach* to turn your thoughts and recollections to the beauty and strength of our ancestral homeland. Invite a friend to share photos and memories of a visit to Israel.

The Sixth Candle: As the Chanukah lights burn, gather a coat, a sweater or blanket to donate to a homeless shelter, or collect canned or packaged food to donate to a food drive.

The Seventh Candle: In anticipation of the seventh night have your grandchildren create handmade *tzedakah* boxes and with your little ones, place them in each room of your home so they will be available for collecting loose change.

The Eighth Candle: Gather family and friends and formally rededicate the rooms of your home so they can better accomplish their sacred tasks--the dining room for guests, the kitchen for sustaining life, the living room for family interaction, the bedroom for rest and intimacy. Obtain additional *mezuzot* and with your friends and family affix these on each entry way. If you have young grandchildren, affix two mezuzot; one placed down low for little ones to touch.

Like Polly said, Chanukah sometimes comes early, with the first candle kindled on or near Thanksgiving Day! Other years Chanukah coincides with the school year's winter holiday. If you are fortunate enough to live near your family or if their schedules permit a visit, you can plan your *Chanukah HaBayit* festivities by inviting children and grandchildren to your home. If not, try gathering the family via Zoom or Skype.

If you live in a retirement community you can share these activities with your friends by selecting one apartment for each of the eight nights. And remember, no worries if you are not permitted to use candles and matches. An electric menorah will do nicely!

Gleanings and Meanings:

1. Why is Chanukah one of the most celebrated of all the Jewish holidays?

2. Which one of the eight rededication ideas would you like to incorporate into your next Chanukah celebration?

3. Why is the mezuzah so important to the Chanukah rededication idea?

Jews and Jingle Bells: Sharing the Holiday with Christian Friends

"It's the time of year when the world falls in love..." Beautiful words for a beautiful time. Christmas time. Not my time of the year but I like it just the same. Surprised? I'm sure some of you must be, especially since I'm Jewish and not only that, I'm a rabbi as well.

That being said, I want to tell you two things. First, Jews don't dislike Christmas. And second, even though we don't observe the holiday, we are glad that Christians do.

December has always been a challenging time for me as a Jew and as the mother of a Jewish child. Anyone who is a member of any minority group probably will tell you the same thing. It's sometimes very hard to be different.

At Christmas, Jews are part of a tiny minority of people who often do not embrace practices and customs that almost the entire country has adopted and made into a national tradition. We're on our own, celebrating Chanukah, which is a minor Jewish holiday, while we're exposed, sometimes for weeks on end, to the hoopla surrounding the observance of another religion. For our children it can be confusing. For us grown-ups it can be exhausting. But for the most part, we Jews aren't distressed about it. Many of us enjoy being guests at your party.

And that's how I approach the "December Dilemma" with my family. In his book, "The Art of Jewish Living," Dr. Ron Wolfson comments on toddlers and how they behave at birthday celebrations. When the cake is brought to the table, all the other children try to blow out the candles along with the birthday boy or girl. As the gifts are opened, each child reaches for the toys. Wolfson tells us that that's why party favors were invented. To teach children the important lesson of "This belongs to you and that belongs to her." Children learn the difference, Wolfson says, between celebrating one's very own birthday and celebrating another's.

Wolfson applies this message to Jewish families and Christmas. Christmas is someone else's party, not ours. Just as we can appreciate someone else's birthday party, just as we can admire the gifts and decorations, just as we can eat the cake and maybe even take a token gift home with us, and, most important, just as we can be happy for them, so too, can we marvel at the beauty of the Christmas season. But it is not our party. It belongs to someone else.

As I walk around the mall, scoot into the grocery store, and pop into the dry cleaners, I notice something interesting about the

Christmas season. Most people are in a good mood. They're dropping dollars into the Salvation Army kettle, they're filling "Adopt A Family" food baskets, they're more patient with their kids and they're smiling at one another. There is less violence on television and more "family specials." The songs on the radio share thoughts of peace, brotherhood and good will.

If the national focus on Christmas is responsible for this annual positive change in behavior, then I'm all for it.

It's ironic but when it comes to Christmas, religious Jews and religious Christians agree on one very important idea. When we hear our Christian friends say, "It's time to put "Christ" back into Christmas," we understand what they mean. Like them, we feel that when a religious holiday is secularized, when commercialism takes the place of religious observance, and when it's more about stuff than substance, then we are all hurt. Christian families are hurt by the assault of the secular on the religious. Jews are hurt because it becomes easier to adopt holiday rituals when those rituals have lost their religious significance and now appear to be neutral.

So what do we do about Christmas? For many Jews we appreciate your invitations to join you for neighborhood parties and share in holiday gift exchanges. We like it when you send us a Chanukah greeting or a card that wishes us "Happy Holidays."

And when you sing carols around the piano, we're not offended. It's your party. If we're friends or even family members, we're happy you asked us to join you.

It can be awkward if you ask our children if they're waiting for Santa. Instead, if you're not sure whether a child is Christian, Jewish, Buddhist, Muslim, or something else, you might say instead, "What do you like best about this time of the year?" And if you want to give a present, that's fine. It's just like a party favor. We all enjoy your thoughtfulness.

So, to all our friends in the Christian community, we Jews wish you a happy holiday season. We wish you and your families a season of peace, understanding and joy. For these are the very same things we pray for in our synagogues each week and work toward in our Jewish communities every day. Our families join yours in the belief that love for and peace between all people can happen in our time. And we applaud your celebration of values and ethics that apply to all people of goodwill everywhere. Merry Christmas!

Gleanings and Meanings:

1. As a Jewish person, how do you approach the Christmas season?

2. Do you attend Christmas gatherings? Why or Why not?

3. Have you ever shared the Christmas holiday with friends or family members? What are the advantages or disadvantages for doing so?

Do Politics From the Bimah Keep Older Jews at Home?

"It's more than I can take," says Harriet, a resident of a Jewish retirement community on Florida's east coast. *"At dinner it's all politics all the time. On the bus to the mall, more politics. I used to enjoy going to my local shul but when the sermons got political and people started arguing ... and when my gentleman friend nearly got into a fist fight at the kiddush, that's when I said, 'Genug! (Enough). I'm staying home."*

I have the opportunity and pleasure to speak to many seniors, often on two continents, so at a recent gathering when this issue came up I was astounded at the emotion the subject evoked. Harriet's opinion, admittedly one of the more extreme, was only one of many voiced by older Jewish men and women, the majority of whom expressed the hope that political talk would be left at the synagogue door.

In our tradition we are taught that Shabbat offers us Jews an opportunity to separate the material concerns of everyday life from a once a week opportunity to focus on spirituality, or as another of my elderly friends put it, "Leave alone the things of the hands. Give yourself time to consider the things of the heart."

In fact in the Conservative movement's Siddur Sim Shalom, we find the following prayer that serves as a Shabbat guide: *Grant me the privilege of the liberating joy of Shabbat... May I be undisturbed by sadness, sorrow or sighing during the holy hours of Shabbat."*

For many shul-going Jews, especially those seniors for whom attendance at services requires more prep time and physical stamina than in years past, more and more elderly congregants find that a recap of the news of the day, replete with tragedy, natural disasters, government shake-ups, terrorism and verbal bashing by politicians and pundits has become outright disturbing. Television news has become so steeped in *Lashon Hara* and vindictive language, often punctuated by curse words and vulgarity, that many Jews share my friend Arthur's opinion when he says, "The last thing I want to do is hear a political sermon that recaps all that I've been bombarded with throughout the week."

Rabbi David Wolpe, of Sinai Temple in Los Angeles, seems to agree. In an article written for the LA Jewish Journal, (June 7, 2017), *"Why I Keep Politics Off the Pulpit,"* Rabbi Wolpe had this to say: "Many people privately ask about my political views and I'm happy to answer, but not from the bimah. As a rabbi, my task is to bless, to teach values and texts and ideas and rituals, to

comfort, to cajole, to listen and learn, to grow in spirit along with my congregants, to usher them through the transitions of life, to create a cohesive community, to defend the people and land of Israel, and to reinforce what most matters."

Tiffany Shlain, founder of "Unplugged for Shabbat," shares this view. In a March 2, 2017 article that appeared in the Jewish Forward, *"Do Yourself a Favor: Unplug This Shabbat,"* Shlain writes that since the last presidential election, upsetting news alerts, emails, tweets and Facebook posts "come at us even more furiously than before." Not to mention 24/7, non-stop cable news.

Shlain sites a recent Nielsen study that reports that the average screen time for American adults is a whopping 74 hours a week and that the majority of those hours are stress related. In fact the Nielson Report expanded its study to include the age span of current cable TV news viewers. "According to Nielsen Live … in 2017 CNN's median age was 60, while the median age of the Fox News and MSNBC viewer was 65." As the population ages those numbers will climb.

A cultural Jew who describes herself as "not religious," Shlain has unplugged and taken a Technology Shabbat each week for several years and describes the experience as "a secret force field of protection to give me the strength, perspective, and energy for the other six days."

Many Jews agree that Shabbat is about meditation, reflection and behavior change. It's about renewing our spiritual selves and promising to revitalize our relationships with our families, our friends and with the God of our understanding. The siddur prayer is an echo emanating from the hearts of many congregants. *"May I be undisturbed by sadness, sorrow or sighing..."* In other words, "May I please turn off the world just for a little while."

Looking inward rather than outward can be "the liberating joy of Shabbat." Or as Rabbi Wolpe puts it, "The great questions of life are not usually political ones." If that's true then messages from the bimah that focus on the politics of the day, could result in our congregants' losing the deep spiritual meaning of what is basic to our Jewish tradition, the peace and tranquility of Shabbat.

Gleanings and Meanings:

1. What is your opinion regarding rabbis offering politically themed sermons?

2. In a recent advertisement for a new rabbi a congregation wrote that "political conservatives need not apply." What is your opinion of this advertisement?

3. If you frequent a synagogue or if you think you might do so, does the political position of the rabbi and/or members factor in your choice? Why or why not?

What Makes Jews So Smart?

"I'm pooped!" Natalie collapsed into her easy chair and fanned herself with her ever-present apron as she recounted her latest trip "up north." "My son, he's an editor and my daughter, she's a photographer with some of her pictures in National Geographic, and their children, what can I tell you? My granddaughter just graduated from medical school and my grandson got accepted to a top law school. The youngest one, he just won first place in his high school science fair. And I'm not the only one '*kvelling*' over how my kids and grandkids made good. My friends could tell you the same stories. So I'm asking, what makes us Jews so smart?"

Natalie's question is not a new one. In fact, if Nobel Prize winners are any indication, we Jews, a tiny minority of the world's population, have been among the best and the brightest for decades. In fact JINFO.org reports that between 1901 and 2018 at least 203 Jewish men and women have won the Nobel Prize, a number that represents 22 percent of all the individual recipients.

When we look at Nobel statistics specific to the United States, in particular in the fields of Chemistry, Economics, Physics and Medicine, 39 percent of Nobel winners are Jewish –

an accomplishment made even more significant given that Jews are only .02 percent of the world's population.

Then there are recent genetic studies, reported by Lazar Berman of the American Enterprise Institute who writes, "There is ample scholarly work to suggest that Ashkenazi Jews, at least, have significantly higher IQs than surrounding populations. In "Natural History of Ashkenazi Intelligence," Gregory Cochran, Jason Hardy, and Henry Harpending of the University of Utah conclude that "Ashkenazi Jews have the highest average IQ of any ethnic group for which there are reliable data."

Setting aside what some might term "the genetic minefield", most parents and teachers, sociologists and scientists agree that for native intelligence to manifest in accomplishment, it must be recognized, nurtured and appreciated. In fact renowned psychologist and author Daniel Goleman in his book, "Emotional Intelligence" notes that a high IQ does not always lead to a successful career. The "EQ" or the Emotional Intelligence Quotient, which includes traits such as optimism, determination, perseverance and ability to work cooperatively with others, plays an important part in a child's eventual success – traits inherent in Bar and Bat Mitzvah preparation and celebration.

Could the answer to Natalie's question about how smart we Jews seem to be, be found in one of our oldest Jewish traditions?

Having prepared dozens of students and officiated at 181 ceremonies I suggest that the Bar/Bat Mitzvah journey plays a critical role in the success our children have later in life.

Boys become Bar Mitzvah at 13 years of age; girls at age 12 and both begin their studies during one of life's most awkward periods – the early teen, middle school years. Much has been written about the emotional turmoil inherent in this period but it doesn't take a sociologist to observe that standing out in a crowd, speaking before a group, or having any of a myriad obvious differences, can create emotional havoc for young teens.

Yet it is right at this developmental stage when Jewish boys and girls are required to set these obstacles aside and ascend the *bimah,* to read from the Torah scroll (in another language, no less) and give a speech on the meaning of an ancient text.

Dr. Thomas G. Plant (Psychology Today) suggests that, because the benefits are so great, not only Jewish teens but all teens should have a Bar or Bat Mitzvah. Dr. Plant, a Catholic, has attended many Bar/Bat Mitzvah celebrations and he writes, "I wish that all religious traditions offered some variation on the theme of a bar/bat mitzvah. It is a remarkable opportunity for a young teen to carefully learn much about their religious tradition, have the chance to lead many parts of a serious and sacred religious service, and give a thoughtful sermon reflecting on scared scripture."

Dr. Plant speaks to the benefits when he concludes that the ceremony "sends the message to the teen that there are many adults taking an interest in his or her development. It is a chance for the youth to become a more responsible and thoughtful member of the religious community (and) if we expect much from our youth in terms of ethics, thoughtfulness, and responsibility, we might actually get it."

Not only does the Bar/Bat Mitzvah experience represent a transition from childhood to young adulthood, the entire process from preparation to party gives our Jewish teens a tremendous sense of accomplishment at a critical time in their emotional development.

In middle school old ideas and behaviors are replaced by new ones and decisions are made to go along with the crowd or to stand apart. The Bar/Bat Mitzvah experience facilitates mental and emotional development at a time when our teens need it most. "Why are we Jews so smart?" Natalie asks. For me the answer lies in one of our most treasured traditions – becoming a Bar or Bat Mitzvah.

Gleanings and Meanings:

1. Do you agree that in general Jews are highly intelligent? Why or why not?

2. Do you think that the Bar Mitzvah experience is a factor in college and/or career success?

3. Jews are often called "The People of the Book." Is this a myth or a contributing factor to academic success?

Ritual Rescue – What Happens to Judaica When Our Kids Don't Want It?

In her article *"My Obsession with Buying Abandoned Jewish Objects,"* author Linda Pressman describes how she found herself immersed into what I like to call "Ritual Rescue," – saving discarded Jewish ritual items. Pressman writes, "It first happened right after I got married. I was at a rundown antique mall and there it was: someone's abandoned brass menorah, with Hebrew written on it, and made in Israel. The sales tag said only, 'Candelabra.' I bought it."

Thus began Ms. Pressman's rescue efforts, propelled in part by her Holocaust survivor parents and grandparents. They were forced from their homes by the Nazis, who stole not only the family's Judaica treasures, but their attachment to Jewish observance as well.

Pressman puts it this way; "As a college student I literally had to claw my way back into my own religion and raise myself Jewish." Scouring second hand and antique stores for Jewish "stuff," helped Pressman capture a tradition that, for her, was nearly lost forever.

I can relate. In my more than 20 years as a rabbi a majority of those years were spent serving older Jewish congregants. Many of these elder Jews had collected dozens of Jewish ritual items, from drawers full of Bar and Bat Mitzvah commemorative kippot to ornate Shabbat candelabra, Havdalah sets and wine-stained, deeply creased tallitot that prior to making the journey to the local Good Will store, often ended up in my hands.

"I'm downsizing," said Ellen, a 90 year old who was about to move into a retirement community. "I tried to give my husband's *tallis* and *tfillin* to my son, but he didn't want them. I just couldn't throw them into the give-away box, so I brought them to you."

And Ellen wasn't the only one. Over the years elderly Jews have brought me Shabbat candlesticks, ornate Chanukah menorahs, battered Kiddush cups, and a shoebox filled with an entire collection of *mezuzot* from around the world! And even though I'm running out of storage space, with love and gratitude I accept them all.

Like author Linda Pressman, I also scour the Good Will and second hand stores and when I find a hand engraved Kiddush cup (one said, "Baruch ben Yosef 1955"), a "Shalom" wall plaque or a tattered matzah cover, I buy them all.

Ironically, as a board member for an international Jewish organization, Kulanu (Hebrew for "all of us"), I have the opportunity to assist emerging Jewish communities in isolated areas of the world. In this capacity I am able to send discarded American Judaica to congregations like those in Uganda, Madagascar and Nicaragua. In addition I often bring these items to members of my own congregation in southern Italy – all of whom are enormously appreciative to receive them.

But these gifts do not solve the problem of what to do about family Judaica that children or grandchildren don't want. For those of us who are holding on to Bubby's seder plate or Zayde's tallit there are some steps we can take to keep our Jewish family heirlooms in our families.

Start by taking your Judaica out of the box, freshen it and display it in your home. That means taking Zayde's tallis to the dry cleaner or having your care giver help you polish the brass Chanukah menorah. When your Judaica looks loved and cared-for, your pride in your heritage will be obvious to your family. Then you can take time to explain the significance of this displayed Judaica to your grandchildren and great grands.

For example, weave a story around Zayde's tallit: "I remember when your great grandfather wore this on Rosh HaShanah. I liked to sit next to him and play with the fringes..." Personalize your Judaica with happy memories and your family members will want to embrace those memories by bringing the long lost Judaica into their homes.

If you have no one to whom you can pass on a treasured Kiddush cup, seder plate or spice box, share your items with a local synagogue that welcomes Jews by Choice. Often someone who has converted to Judaism does not have family treasures and would appreciate bringing your Judaica into her/his family.

Last year in a local Good Will store I found a very old Kiddush cup. It sat on a shelf crowded with an assortment of pewter and silver goblets and was so tarnished that I nearly missed the inscriptions. Engraved on the cup, complete with a delicate Magen David, were the names of three generations of Bar Mitzvah boys and the dates of their celebrations. The cup was nearly 100 years old.

Sad as it was to see where this treasure ended up, my Ritual Rescue instinct kicked in and I brought the Kiddush cup home. Now I use it for Bar and Bat Mitzvah celebrations, encouraging our Italian boys and girls whose families are reclaiming their Jewish roots, to lift the cup, make the blessing and give new life to a tradition one family has lost, but for others has been rediscovered and embraced.

In ancient times our sages encouraged *"hiddur mitzvah,"* which means taking the time and making the effort to enrich our

Jewish ceremonies with the most beautiful ritual objects we can find. Many of these gorgeous items now hide in storage bins or sit forlorn on second hand store shelves, just waiting for a family's attention once more. From your table to your descendants' table, to a convert's table to the rickety table in an emerging congregation – ritual rescue can bring our Judaica back to life.

Gleanings and Meanings:

1. As Jews become more culturally or secularly oriented, are ritual items losing their importance and/or meaning?

2. Do you have ritual items at home that you plan on sharing with friends and/or family members? Who will you give them to and why?

3. If our children or grandchildren haven't shown interest in preserving our family's Jewish ritual items, how can we change their opinions? Should we try?

PART II:

Relationships

"Love your neighbor as yourself." Leviticus 19:18

Interfaith Grandkids and Crayola Crayons

"Rabbi, I have to ask you something and it's very personal," said Ann as she wagged her finger in the typical "don't tell," motion. At the time of her question Ann was a relative newcomer at her Jewish retirement community and she was still learning the intricacies of her new home.

"Of course," I responded, "Let's do lunch right here in our own bistro." Ann demurred. "Thanks, Rabbi but I want to talk with you where I'll be sure that no one can hear us, OK?" We agreed to meet later on that day in the privacy of Ann's apartment.

Stirring my cup of tea at Ann's table, I broached the subject. "Ann, "I asked, "What is it that seems to be troubling you so?" Clearing the cups from the table, Ann paused then asked, "Do you remember Crayola Crayons? When we were kids everyone had them."

In a flash Ann brought me back to second grade. "I sure do," I said. "I'll always remember 'burnt sienna!"

"All those colors," Ann mused. "That's what I have to talk to you about."

The quizzical look on my face must have had an effect, prompting Ann to explain. "Crayola Crayons, that's what I call my family. My children, their spouses, my grandchildren, my whole *meshpucha* are the crayons in one big crayon box!"

As I looked around Ann's apartment I began to understand. Beautifully framed photos were displayed on shelves and table tops, each one featuring individual close ups or large and small family groups.

"There they are," Ann said proudly. "My crayons. My daughter there is married to a Korean man. So look! I have Asian grandchildren, four of them. My son is married to a doctor from Kenya so those grandkids are part African. My other son and his wife adopted two girls, one from Thailand and the other from Ethiopia. My family has more colors than Crayola!"

As Ann returned the family photos to their original places I couldn't help but ask, "Ann, you have a beautiful family. What's the problem?"

And that's when Ann opened the door to her fears. As a full time resident in Independent Living for just under two months she was concerned about family visits. "It's obvious that my family is mixed and that my children 'married out.' When they come to visit how will it be? Do you think the people here will accept my 'crayons'?"

For a person from Ann's generation the question is a legitimate one, especially when we look at the statistics on interfaith families. Nearly 50 years ago when Ann was newly married, the rate of intermarriage between Jews and gentiles was 17%.

Quite possibly Ann's concerns stem from her memories of how unusual interfaith marriages were back then. Ann might even remember that very few rabbis would officiate at interfaith weddings and some families refused to accept their son or daughter's non-Jewish spouse.

Over the years as acceptance and appreciation of diversity has become the norm in American culture, interfaith families benefited from this sociological shift. In the 1990's interfaith marriages rose to 43 percent of all Jewish marriages, a figure that is more than double the 1960's numbers. Today, according to the most recent Pew Research Report, the overall intermarriage rate is 58 percent.

What this means for Ann and others with "Crayola Crayon" families is that the stigma of the interfaith couple is virtually gone. Rather than "marrying out," the idea of "marrying in" has become the term of choice when discussing pairings, especially since 62 percent of Pew's young Jewish adult respondents said that being Jewish is primarily a matter of ancestry and culture."

In only six weeks after our meeting when Ann and I discussed her fears regarding her "crayon" kids, Ann had the opportunity to experience firsthand the open and loving environment that characterizes her new Jewish community. It was Passover week and visiting families packed the common area. Ann's children and grandchildren were visiting as well and Ann was beaming at that warm welcome and loving attention residents gave to each one of Ann's clan. Grandchildren with roots from cultures all over the world, put down new roots as they climbed on the laps of the bubbys and zaydes they had just met.

"Do you know my bubby?" Edye from Ethiopia asked the centenarian sitting beside her on the sofa. In a flash little Edye was pulling her grandmother, Ann, and her little Asian cousin toward her new friend. "My cousin can sing a song in Korean. Want to hear it?"

And Ann? Well, she was beaming, secure in the knowledge that her new community was loving toward and accepting of everyone, including her own "Crayola Crayon" family. "We're a lot of crayon colors" Ann said, "and now I've got a new crayon box. It's so good to know that for all of us, we fit right in!"

Gleanings and Meanings:

1. Do you or your friends have interfaith or ethnically diverse children or grandchildren? If so, how are they accepted both within and outside of the family?

2. How important are interfaith and ethnic and racial diversity issues to Judaism today?

3. Do you see a change in the acceptance of interfaith marriages among Jewish denominations? If so, how has the situation changed over the years? Are these changes helpful or harmful to traditional Judaism?

Sharing Jewish Heritage with Interfaith and Secular Grandchildren

"I'm afraid to interfere," said Magda, grandmother to interfaith twin girls whose Jewish son and Methodist daughter-in-law are raising their daughters in both faiths.

Magda's friend "Zayde" Nathan shares her concerns. Nathan says, "My grandson is almost ten and I haven't brought up the Jewish thing. His parents are atheists and refer to themselves as cultural Jews, but they don't do anything Jewish. I won't be here forever. I want my grandson to know about his Jewish roots."

With a Unite States intermarriage rate at nearly 60 percent, and with more than 30 percent of Jews self- identifying as non-observant or secular, it seems that Grandma Magda and Zayde Nathan's concerns are not unique. For more than one third of American Jewish families, issues regarding how and when to share Jewish traditions are a sensitive part of the grand-parenting experience.

One of the first to describe the joys and challenges facing interfaith grandparents was author Sunie Levin. In her groundbreaking book, *Mingled Roots – A Guide for Jewish*

Grandparents of Interfaith Children (UAHC Press, 2003). Levin shares her personal experiences with the topic.

As a rabbi who supports intermarriage and the uniquely rich trove of traditions that characterizes so many interfaith families, I've applied Levin's perspective to encourage Jewish grandparents to share their heritage with the grandkids.

Where to begin? First, some ground rules. Ancient Jewish practice dictates that we Jews do not proselytize, meaning that we don't actively try to convert others to become Jews. This rule applies to our grandchildren, too. Depending on your family's Jewish denomination, you may already consider that your grandchildren are Jewish, but modern life demonstrates that Jewishness is less about bloodline and more about day to day behavior.

Respect is key. You may not agree with the religious climate (or lack of it) in your grandkids' home, but if you adopt an attitude that demonstrates respect for their choices, interfaith and secular parents may be more open to grandparents' sharing family history with their children.

The grandkids may understand that mom or dad is Jewish but it's possible that they have had no experience with the history and traditions of the Jewish people. That's where the grandparents come in. As bearers of the flame, grandparents are the family members who give the youngest generation a sense of their history. So it doesn't matter if the grandkids are part of shul-going family or if they are being raised in a Christian or secular environment, grandparents can play an important role in helping their grandkids appreciate who they are and where they come from.

Here are some things that you can do.

The Mini-Museum

Create a Jewish corner in your own home. Shine the Chanukah menorah and buy some Shabbat candles. Find the family *kiddush* cup and great-grandpa's *tallit*. Select a spot for your mini-museum, making sure that it is eye-level for the little ones. Ask your Jewish son or daughter if she/he would like to contribute a personal item to the "museum," as well.

When the grandchildren visit, show them their family museum, let them explore, touch and ask questions. Personalize the items. "This is my father's tallit and these were my mother's Shabbat candlesticks." Or if these items are no longer accessible, adapt – "This is a tallit like my father wore and these are candlesticks just like my mother had for Shabbat." Before each visit add an item or two and ask your grandchild if she can find what's new in the mini-museum. When the kids are familiar with the items, organize a scavenger hunt to foster a personal hands-on relationship with your family's Jewish treasures.

Nothin' Says Lovin' like Jewish cooking

If you are able to spend time with your grandchildren, create a cooking school experience. Use family recipes for brisket, latkes, kugel or blintzes and teach the grandkids how to become chefs in Bubby's Jewish Cooking School. While you're creating, be sure to share family memories of how, when and why these Jewish foods were eaten. Invite the parents to sample the feast.

Jewish Holidays

Passover is the Jewish holiday celebrated by more Jews than any other. Regardless of Jewish persuasion the Passover *seder* (traditional meal with symbolic foods, prayers and stories) has brought more *Yiddishkeit* to interfaith and secular families than any other holiday experience. With this in mind, have your grandchildren help you organize the seder by creating individual seder plates, matzah covers or book covers for the Haggadah.

Chanukah ranks as the second most popular Jewish holiday, even more special because it has its own unique interfaith meaning. Kindling the candles and placing the lighted menorah in the window demonstrates the basic tenet of the festival – religious freedom. An interfaith or secular family is an example of religious tolerance and appreciation of differences. Making or buying individual Chanukah menorahs for each family member can add to the enjoyment and, if you've made your "Mini Museum," they can be enjoyed the year round.

UK's Rabbi Gideon Sylvester puts it well when he discusses teaching about Judaism to anyone, Jewish or not (Jewish Chronicle 2010). Rabbi Sylvester references the Torah where it says, *"Keep my commandments which a person should perform and through which they will gain eternal life"* (Leviticus 18: 5). The verse makes no distinction between Jews and non-Jews - Torah is there for everyone, including our interfaith and secular grandkids.

Gleanings and Meanings:

1. How proactive should grandparents be in sharing Jewish traditions with interfaith or secular grandchildren?

2. Is there a difference in a focus on Jewish culture versus Jewish religion? If so, how should grandparents make this distinction?

3. How important is it to pass on Jewish traditions to the next generation?

Getting Divorced Kids through the Holidays

Each year kids everywhere are excited for the holiday vacations that encompass Chanukah and Christmas. But for many children whose parents are divorced, the holiday season can be at best difficult and at worst traumatic. Getting divorce kids through the holiday season may require a little extra attention.

Before I became a rabbi, I served on the board of a counseling service for divorced families. Later, when I became a rabbi, I became a support group leader and counselor to families and children who suffer through all the issues surrounding the breakup of a marriage. I've seen a lot. From my own experience as a divorced parent to my work as a counselor, I've come to the conclusion that the most difficult divorces involve children and the areas that are most contentious surround child support, custody and visitation. And each of these is exacerbated when the holidays roll around.

Acknowledging that the holiday season can be a particularly stressful time of the year for divorced kids, what can we parents and grandparents do to assure that "happy holidays" is more than just a song on the radio?

Several years ago, when my daughter, R. was a young adult, I asked her to tell me the things her father and I did right as well as those things we did wrong. Here are my daughter's eight holiday suggestions for divorced families.

Don't fight about schedules

Be flexible. Remember that what is drafted in a legal document often doesn't represent real situations, especially as children grow. R. suggests that both parents discuss a holiday schedule and, include older children (nine and up) in the decision making. But my daughter cautioned that parents should not make their child feel guilty about the choices she makes. "Staying an extra day with you or Daddy didn't mean I loved one of you more than the other. It just meant that's what was easiest for me. I needed you both to respect my opinions. Parents can really wreck a holiday by putting the "legal" schedule ahead of what makes sense for the child.

Let Your Child Bring a Friend

For the non-custodial parent, let your kids bring friends over. Friends are so important and holidays are great times for friendships to develop. It can be lonely for a kid to go to Dad's (or Mom's) and be the only child among grown-ups. Remember that inviting a friend along doesn't detract from the visit. Often it enhances it. R. says, "My best holidays with my dad were when he let my best girlfriend share a vacation day with me."

Encourage Your Child to Select Gifts for your Ex and her/his Parents, too

"Help your child select, buy and wrap gifts for the other parent. Ouch! Really? That's what my daughter said. "On this one you did well, Mom. You took me out to buy my dad's birthday and Chanukah gifts and made sure I wrapped them nicely and sent a card. Especially when I was little, I was so happy that I had my own present to take to my dad.

Let your child relax

That seems like a simple idea, but once again, my child-of-divorce emphasizes that this is a big area that is often over looked. Divorced kids spend a lot of time going back and forth between parents. R. recalls, "I appreciated spending the whole day of a holiday at home. It was exhausting to get up early, run to Dad's, then race home for the second half of the day with Mom. One New Year's Day I spent most of it in the car. It was awful!"

Now I understand that although the lawyers recommended it, counting holiday hours and strictly dividing them in half was not in our child's best interest. As parents we needed to communicate. Rather than creating happy memories, we contributed to her stress and upset.

When it comes to gifts, don't compete and don't comment

This was a particularly sore spot for my daughter, who, years later, remembers the argument she overheard between her father and me about who was going to purchase her first bicycle. "What should have been a wonderful memory was wrecked by you two fighting about my present," R. says.

I admit it. I really goofed on this one. Not only did I resist my ex-husband's offer that we purchase the gift it together, but I made snide comments about our financial situation. To this day my daughter's memory of her favorite Chanukah gift is tainted by my self-centered "Victim Queen" behavior. On other occasions I made negative comments about gifts R. received from her father and his friends. I'm ashamed to say that one year my daughter hid these presents rather than risk my remarks. That should never happen.

Never say bad things about the other parent

My daughter says, "No matter how you feel, be a grown-up and remember that your first duty is to be a good parent. And good parents don't say nasty things about each other. Ever."

Most divorced children report that this is the one area where the most harm is most consistently done. One seven year old child recalls, "When my mom said my dad was bad, then I felt like half of me was bad. And when my dad said the same thing about my mom, then I felt like all of me was bad!" Bad- mouthing each other is the quickest, most effective way to ruin your child's self esteem, not only during the holidays but throughout the year. A child who is encouraged to hate a parent will end up hating her/himself in the process.

Holidays are family time. Bite your tongue, swallow your pride and do one thing together as a family

I was surprised how important this was to my daughter. She said, "The time you came to my school performance and you both sat together was one of the best holidays I ever had. Usually I had to run back and forth between you and Daddy. But that year, you did the work, instead of making me do it. You sat together and you greeted me together. I'll never forget how good that felt."

I had no idea that such a little thing would mean so much. And I must be honest and say that I almost didn't do it. My ex's girlfriend was with him and I was alone, annoyed and jealous. The temptation to sulk and stay bitter was almost overwhelming. But a counselor told me that a little effort toward family behavior would make a big difference for my child. I guess I never knew how much.

Other kids say that a holiday meal or even a stop for ice cream shared with mom and dad together are among their fondest memories. And don't forget to include step parents. If you and/or your ex are remarried, your child now must relate to more adults who share the parental role. When you demonstrate your acceptance and respect, your children will follow suit and not feel torn or stressed relating to them. Remember, if you truly want what's best for your child, then you want your ex to be happy. An ex-husband or ex-wife who is happily remarried means that your children will be happy when they are together with their own mom or dad.

Grandparents are very important

My daughter says, "You always let me see my Nana. Even though she didn't like you anymore, you didn't try to punish her by keeping me away from my grandma."

You may have divorced your child's parent, but your children did not divorce grandma and grandpa. Research indicates that the more contact children have with loving members of their extended families, the healthier human beings they become. Because you're angry or disappointed with your ex, it may seem like a good idea to punish your former spouse by restricting your child's contact with your ex's parents. Do that and you hurt your own child as well.

So, Happy Chanukah, Merry Christmas and Happy Holidays to you and yours. And if "yours" happens to include ex-spouses, step parents and blended families, remember that holiday celebrations bring with them special challenges. If you haven't done so yet, this year rise to the occasion. Be more gracious, open and loving than you ever have been before. Your children will thank you and respect you for it.

Gleanings and Meanings:

1. Do you or any of your friends have grandchildren whose parents are divorced? If so, what are some of the joys and challenges that these families face?

2. How proactive should grandparents be when co-parenting arrangements and schedules are organized by divorcing spouses?

3. Many child psychologists believe that grandparents provide a "safe haven" for children, especially when their parents' divorce is contentious. Do you agree or disagree? Why or why not?

Jews and Tattoos

Not long ago I received a call from a grieving widow. Her beloved husband of 71 years had passed away. "Jake wasn't all that religious," his wife Arlene explained, "but I do know that he wanted a Jewish funeral in a Jewish cemetery. I was making arrangements when my brother-in-law phoned to tell me that Jake's Jewish funeral was impossible." Arlene was shocked. Then Jake's brother explained. He said "Jake can't be buried in a Jewish cemetery because when Jake was in the Navy he got a tattoo."

These days, tattoos are all the rage. Among the general public there are those who view the tattoo as an artistic or even a spiritual expression, yet others are opposed to any activity that permanently marks the body. For us Jews however, the tattoo issue has deeply historical an emotional significance.

Turning to the Torah in VaYikra (Leviticus) we find a specific prohibition regarding tattoos: *"You shall not make gashes in your flesh for the dead, or incise any marks on yourselves: I am the Lord"* (Leviticus 19:28).

Even Maimonides, one of greatest commentators, had a tattoo opinion. He concluded that regardless of intent, the act of tattooing is prohibited (Mishneh Torah, Laws of Idolatry 12:11). Then there's Professor Aaron Demsky of Bar-Ilan University who sites text from Isaiah and Job that suggests that tattooing was acceptable in biblical times.

A modern perspective comes from a tattooed rabbi himself. Rabbi Marshal Klaven of Congregation B'nai Israel in Texas got his first tattoo at 16 years of age and now boasts four more, each depicting a Jewish theme.

Rabbi Klaven even wrote his rabbinic thesis on tattooing in Jewish history. "In the Torah, tattoos marking affiliation to the people of Israel and/or the God of Israel were accepted, if not encouraged, more times than not," says the rabbi who adds, "In the classic rabbinic period, what bothered the rabbis was not the presence or the content of that mark, but its intended purpose."

While a minority of sages believed that willfully receiving or giving a tattoo was a transgression, the majority objected only when the tattoo served an idolatrous purpose." (Carol Kemp, "Rethink the Ink," Jewish News Online UK 2017))

Regardless of the historical argument, the emotional impact of tattooing is not lost on Holocaust survivors, their children and even their grandchildren. Historians tell us that during the Holocaust, (1941-42) concentration camp prisoners received tattoos only at the Auschwitz concentration camp complex, that included Auschwitz I (Main Camp), Auschwitz II (Auschwitz-Birkenau), and Auschwitz III (Monowitz and the sub camps).

The procedure was brutal and dehumanizing. Eye witness accounts from survivors testify to a procedure that featured "a special metal stamp, holding interchangeable numbers made up of needles ... which allowed the whole serial number to be punched at one blow onto the prisoner's left upper chest. Ink was then rubbed into the bleeding wound.

Later on a single-needle device was introduced, which pierced the outlines of the serial-number digits onto the skin." (Tattoos and Numbers, US Holocaust Museum)

There is no record of a tattooed Holocaust survivor having been denied burial in a Jewish cemetery. In fact many modern rabbis including eight scholars polled for an article on the topic say that the burial prohibition for a tattooed Jew is an urban legend most likely started because a specific cemetery had a policy against tattoos.

Even Chabad spokesperson, Chani Benjaminson states "The Torah forbids us from tattooing our bodies. Nonetheless, one who has had tattoos can still be buried in a Jewish cemetery." So where did the prohibition come from? It's likely that Jewish parents and grandparents, many of whom found tattoos distasteful, passed off the myth as Jewish law.

Indeed, Jake's widow, the "Arlene" in our story, had no need to worry. Jake's Navy tattoo would not prohibit a Jewish burial.

That being said, our Holocaust history paints a horrifying picture of tattooing juxtaposed with the cultural phenomenon that nearly 40 percent of our adult children and 36 percent of our teenage grandchildren have at least one tattoo. What does this mean for us Jews? Beyond debunking the cemetery myth, a discussion of Jews and tattoos seems to be one that is quite timely, culturally appropriate, and indeed worth having.

(NOTE: To learn more about denominational perspectives regarding Jews and tattoos see: http://www.momentmag.com/are-tattoos-and-body-piercings-taboo/)

Gleanings and Meanings:

1. What is your opinion of the explosion of tattoos among young people? How do you feel about what some call a cultural phenomenon?

2. Do any of your family members have tattoos? If so how did you react? Did you ignore the tattoo or make a comment?

3. If a grandchild wanted to get a Jewish or religiously themed tattoo would you be supportive? Why or why not?

The Impact of Pet Ownership for Seniors

Their names are Scruffy, Ruffy, Midnight and Puddin'Pie. Then there's Tuvia, Tova, Sheina and Butch. These are the names of dogs and cats - pets whose owners I've come to know and love over the years that I served as a campus and resident rabbi at several Tampa Bay retirement homes. And during those years I had direct experience with what sociologists, psychologists and gerontologists report about senior citizens and pets – specifically it's a fabulous combination that promotes mental and physical health.

In an article by Freedom Ahn that first appeared in the Huffington Post's "Healthy Living" (12/2016) and was reprinted in the publication of the Madlyn and Leonard Abramson Center for Jewish Life, we learn about "The Paw-sitive Effect of Pets," especially for elderly pet owners. Researchers confirm that the health benefits for seniors who have pets include:

Reduction of blood pressure

Reduction of depressed mood by increasing serotonin and dopamine levels

Reduction of visits to a doctor

Increased opportunities to exercise

Opportunity to meet new people

Reduction in loneliness

Yet although the benefits of elderly pet ownership seem obvious, there are misconceptions that abound. For example, Helen is a woman in her 90's who says *"I am in love with my cat. Her name is Tova and I've had her for ages. We're best friends. So I told my daughter, I'm not going into a retirement home. They won't take Tova so they won't have me either!"*

Years ago, before gerontology professionals understood the positive impact of a pet's companionship on an aging senior, most retirement facilities would not accept a resident's cat or dog. But now, with what we know about the health benefits related to pet ownership, the situation has changed for the better.

Thanks to an online clearinghouse, After55.com, it is now possible to find pet friendly senior housing and even pet friendly assisted living facilities all over the United States. In fact **After55.com** reports that a whopping 78% of our senior living communities welcomed pets. They say, "Pet-friendly senior housing units usually allow cats, small- to medium-sized dogs, and other small animals such as birds and fish. Some senior communities have "community" dogs and cats that live on site. A few nursing homes and assisted living facilities even have pet chickens. You may even find a community that offers pet care and grooming among its extra services."

"But what if I get sick? Need an operation? Have to go to the hospital or rehab?" That's the question Art asked as he considered adding a sweet young rescue dog as a live-In companion. *"I want to have a dog,"* Art says, *"But I want to be responsible, too. Who will take my dog if I'm incapacitated?"*

Art's concerns are legitimate ones; which is why "PACT for Animals," was created. PACT is a unique service that matches pets with foster families when the pet owner needs someone to care longer term for a dog or cat.

Originally designed to serve military personnel who faced deployment and needed a long term living solution for a beloved pet, PACT for Animals now offers family fostering opportunities for elderly pet owners who face surgery or rehabilitation.

PACT for Animals reports "(We give) peace of mind to hospital patients and military personnel by placing their pets into temporary foster homes until their owners can be reunited with the devoted companions they love."

Founded in 2011 as the first organization of its kind, PACT has facilitated the placement of more than 700 companion pets nationwide. The service is offered at no charge, however PACT requires the owner to reimburse the foster family for their pet's food, grooming, and medical expenses.

The Senior Solutions Center at Colorado's Jewish Family Services puts it well when they say, "For seniors and those living alone, pets can have a profound impact on quality of life." *Baruch HaShem*, there are now senior housing opportunities that understand this basic principle and organizations such as PACT for Animals that offer help and peace of mind to senior pet owners as they age.

Gleanings and Meanings:

1. Do you agree with the premise of the article that pets have a positive effect on older people?

2. Did you have a pet while you were growing up? Did you children have pets? If so, what are your memories surrounding the pets in your home?

3. If you were feeling isolated or alone would you consider a pet later in life? Why or why not?

When Our Widowed Parents Find Love Again

Several years ago I opened the door to my rabbi's study to find an elderly couple, both well into their eighties, hoping that I would meet with them. At first I thought something terrible had happened. The man hung his head and the woman began to cry. I invited them in to hear what I was certain would be awful news. "Rabbi," the man said, "I don't know how to tell you this but Esther and I want to get married."

I smiled at both of them and offered a hearty Mazel Tov. I looked at Esther and said, "That's wonderful. You're crying tears of joy!" Esther daubed her eyes as tears streamed down her cheeks. Finally she composed herself enough to say, "Sam and I have a very big *tsuris*. Sam's children and my children are against our marriage. They won't even come to our wedding." Sam piped up, "Just wait, Rabbi. Next week you'll hear the whole story. My kids are coming to town and they want to talk to you. They want you to convince us not to get married."

Sam was right. Six days later I found myself cramming extra chairs into my study to accommodate Sam's four adult children each of whom was dead set against their father's relationship with Esther.

The oldest son, functioning as designated spokesperson began. "My sisters and I are really worried about our father. Mom died three years ago and our father could barely cope. He seemed depressed."

Another sister continued, "We suggested he see a therapist. But do you know what he did? He found a girlfriend. They met a year ago and now he thinks he's madly in love!"

"Love!" The younger son spat out the word as though it were straight vinegar. "Her name is Esther and she's nothing like our mother was. She's a gold digger. She wants our father's money."

The children begged for my help. "Don't let him do something stupid," said the eldest boy. "Talk some sense into Dad before it's too late."

"I can see how upset you are," I began, "but I want you to know that I've met your father and I've met Esther, too. They seem devoted to each other. Like your father, Esther owns her own home and she has her own money. But more than that Esther was instrumental in his rejoining life after your mother died. In my opinion Sam and Esther seem like a very good match."

When it became clear that I would not help them alter Sam and Esther's plans, the children left so abruptly that I didn't have the opportunity to share what the Torah tells us about second marriages and how adult children should behave when a parent finds a new spouse.

One of our greatest sages, Rashi himself, speaks about an event that our commentators believe occurred after Sarah's death. They wrote that Isaac journeyed to find a wife for his father - woman named Keturah – whom he escorts back to Abraham's house.

The midrash goes on to explain that this Keturah was most likely Hagar – someone not necessarily beloved in the Isaac household. Yet, although it was a difficult and painful thing for Isaac to do, he set aside his misgivings and served as witness at his father's second wedding.

Isaac loved his mother and was very attached to her, but Isaac also lived by the mitzvah to honor his mother and his father. How? When you help your father rebuild his shattered life, you not only honor him and sustain him, but you also honor your mother. Why? Your mother loved your father, so she would want him to have a happy life.

To the children who balked at their father's relationship with Esther, I suggest that if Isaac could make the trip to bring Hagar to Abraham and then serve as best man at his father's wedding, then they could do the same.

Adult children can draw upon innate love and compassion, with the understanding that individuals thrive when they have someone special in their lives. With love and respect for our widowed parents, we can accept and hopefully celebrate the choices they make.

Gleanings and Meanings:

1. In this article the adult children are concerned about their father's new relationship. Are these concerns justified? Why or why not?

2. Have you or your friends experienced romantic relationships later in life? How did families react?

3. Given their children's misgivings, what advice would you give to Esther and Sam?

When Divorced Parents Age

"When the telephone rang at 2:00 am I knew it had to be bad news... and it was," says Kyle who, along with his older sister, shares the responsibility for caring for their aging parents. "My sister was out of town so I raced to the hospital to be with Mom. She lives alone and that night she fell and broke her hip."

Kyle's mother is not a widow but she lives alone because 27 years ago she and Kyle's father divorced. Now both parents are elderly and both have serious health concerns. "Dad has a bad heart," Kyle says, "and I notice his dementia is getting worse. He has a girlfriend but they never married. Last week when she had chest pains, Dad didn't call her daughter. He called me!

There've been times when my sister and I spend every night of the week running back and forth among the three of them. I love my parents but my "shuttle bus" life is exhausting."

Kyle and his sister are not alone. According to an article by Chris Taylor (Wealth magazine 2012) "Some 60 percent of unmarried boomers are divorced." The implications for the next generation are serious as adult children of divorce struggle with the emotional and financial issues related to what Chris Taylor calls a "demographic tsunami."

Professor Susan Brown co-authored a study that examined the sociological meaning of what gerontologists see as an alarming statistic. Brown reports that the current crop of unmarried boomers "are much more economically vulnerable than married boomers are" – a situation made especially precarious when multiple marriages are involved.

Adult children like Kyle and his sister may find themselves responsible not only for two parents who live miles apart but for their parents' significant other – the stepparent or companion who, like their own mom and dad, eventually needs care and support. When stepsiblings are involved, the situation becomes even more complicated.

Francine Russo, author of "They're Your Parents Too," emphasizes that in addition to the financial stress of two parents with two different living situations, the emotional stakes can be quite high. Russo reports that "Adult children of divorce may feel anger or resentment at one parent, or feel like they have to parse out their time equally between both parents … and it can get pretty intense."

In a recent article by Ashley Rosa, "Late-Life Parental Divorce: How to Care for Your Parents," (DivorceMagazine.com 2019) the author offers suggestions regarding caring for elderly parents, especially when they divorce later in life.

In what she describes as "double trouble," Ms. Rosa notes that the practical support that happily married seniors enjoy often evaporates when seniors divorce, especially after they've postponed the split, sometimes waiting years for their children to become adults before they take steps to dissolve the marriage.

Ms. Rosa reminds us that adult children of divorce and their parents have issues that need to be addressed. She says, "As an adult, you feel that you should be able to cope and you shouldn't feel so emotional about your parents' divorce – making you likely to suffer in silence rather than reaching out for help."

Breaking that silence is critical and Ms. Rosa offers practical suggestions for doing just that:

1. Begin with an honest parent/adult child meeting where emotional issues are acknowledged and addressed.

2. Continue with frank discussions about finances and living arrangements.

3. Speak up about how care-giving responsibilities can be shared with siblings, both natural and step.

4. Make plans for care-giver respite care and for the possibility of care-giver burn out.

In an article on "Divorce Etiquette" (ReformJudaism.org), psychotherapist Edythe Held Mencher and family law specialist

Marsha Elser discuss how the synagogue community can facilitate positive relationships with families who for years have been navigating the troubled waters of divorce.

The authors emphasize that Jewish professionals can play a leading role as they plan programs and support services that acknowledge that a parent's divorce has lifelong emotional impact for the children. At each age and stage, from early childhood through the teen years and on to adulthood, divorce brings with it its own set of psychological concerns. Organizing a Jewish community support group for adult children of elderly divorced parents is one way to ease the isolation that these adults often feel.

Within our Jewish communities divorced seniors are living alone, often with the particular emotional burden that characterizes a family split. At the same time adult children of these seniors struggle with the difficulties of what Kyle calls "the shuttle bus life." Given what the statistics tell us, helping divorced boomers and their adult children is a mitzvah in the making for Jewish communities nationwide.

Gleanings and Meanings:

1. What effect, if any, does a parent's divorce have on the children of aging parents?

2. Do you agree or disagree that adult children of divorced parents have psychological challenges related to parental divorce regardless of when the divorce actually took place? If so what are some of the issues adult children face?

3. If you grew up in a divorced family, how would you advise Kyle and his sister and step siblings?

Sex and Seniors – The Jewish Perspective

Daniel Reingold, president and CEO of River Spring Health, the organization that operates the Hebrew Home of Riverdale, NY, is credited with developing a policy that highlights an important aspect of senior living.

In an article titled "The Jewish Nursing Home Where You're Never Too Old for Sex," (Kveller, July 2016), reporter Joanna C. Valente recounts Mr. Reingold's reaction when he was faced with a particularly delicate issue. "In 1995 after a nurse walked in on two residents having sex, the nurse asked Mr. Reingold what to do … and he infamously told her, "Tiptoe out and close the door behind you."

Reingold's response led to the 1995 establishment of his organization's sexual expression policy. In fact Reingold said, "The policy is meant to protect both those who seek intimacy, and those who receive unwanted advances." Reingold believes strongly that is vitally important that those who work in service to the elderly recognize that "sex is here to stay."

Barbara and Joel (not their real names) would agree. Barbara recalls, "We met at one of the lectures that we have here in our retirement community. The speaker asked for questions and I was impressed with what Joel had to say."

Joel nods a definite "yes." "She came over to me and thanked me for my comment. We made a date to have coffee and the rest is history!"

Barbara and Joel both had lost their spouses and after several years of living alone, they were open to new experiences, new friends and new love. "And that's what we have," says Joel who emphasizes, "Do we have sex? Yes indeed we do!"

Rabbi Michael Gold, author of "Does God Belong in the Bedroom," addresses unmarried sex and offers advice from a Torah point of view. Rabbi Gold writes that although rabbis of the Talmudic period specifically spoke against it, "The written Torah never forbids sex outside the context of marriage, with the exception of adultery and incest. On the contrary, the Torah seems to assume that it is a natural part of life."

Apparently so. In fact Dr. Mehmet Oz and Dr. Mike Roizen, both MDs, cite the National Poll on Healthy Aging that questioned more than 1,000 seniors between age 65 and 80. A full 75 percent said they had a romantic partner and more than half reported that they are sexually active. All well and quite good, except for the fact that senior love and romance includes increased risk.

Recent studies find that among elderly men and women, sexually transmitted diseases are at an all-time high. Medical professionals report that from 2007 to 2012 syphilis has increased 52 percent and the AARP notes that "every year since 2012, there has been about a 20 percent jump in the incidence of STDs." In fact the problem is so pervasive that the AARP reminds seniors that Medicare now offers free STD screenings especially for their age group.

From a Jewish perspective, journalists at My Jewish Learning (MJL) found that among modern rabbis, times have changed. They write that "While most Orthodox and Conservative rabbis do consider sex outside marriage inappropriate, most Reform and Reconstructionist (and some Conservative) rabbis are less severe in their language. The official position of the Reform movement is that sex outside of marriage is not ideal, but it is not considered "forbidden." MJL goes on the say that their findings indicate that few Reconstructionist rabbis would prohibit sex outside of marriage as well.

Thanks to the attitudes of professionals like the Hebrew Home's Daniel Reingold, sex among seniors is a topic that today can be openly acknowledged and discussed, free from embarrassment or shame. Reingold says, "We don't lose the pleasure that comes with touch. If intimacy leads to a sexual relationship, then let's deal with it as grown-ups."

Gleanings and Meanings:

1. Do you agree with the administrator's advice to the staff member who discovered residents having sex? Why or why not?

2. As we age, how important is physical contact?

3. Are there difficulties specific to elderly men and women in finding and maintaining a romantic relationship?

PART III:

RISIBILITY – On the Light Side

"Our mouth was filled with laughter, and our tongue with shouts of joy." Psalm 126:2

Ice Cream's Jewish Connection

It's always a good time to enjoy summertime's favorite treat – ice cream. It's cool, it's delicious and it's Jewish!

Thanks to an article by Joan Nathan (Tablet Magazine) we can start by introducing Reuben Mattus who began his career in the ice cream business in the 1920s when he was only ten years old. That's when little Reuben and his widowed mother, Leah, landed in America. They met up with an uncle who made a living in Brooklyn's lemon ice business and gave mother and son a job.

This was before the invention of the refrigerator and Ruben Mattus recalls, "In those days, we bought the ice from the Great Lakes in the winter and buried it with sawdust in pits in the ground until summer," which is how Mattus was able to made ice pops, chocolate covered ice cream bars and ice cream sandwiches, too.

Reuben Mattus married fellow Polish immigrant, Rose Vesel and together with his mom they perfected their ice cream recipe.

While Rose developed marketing strategies, Ruben set out to create a business name - one that would give them notice and set them apart. That's how these Polish Jewish immigrants created their company name, Häagen-Dazs!

Mattus was inspired by Jewish history. He knew that one of the few countries that actively saved Jews during World War II was Denmark, so to honor Demark's courage Mattus created a totally fictitious Danish name and had it registered. When he was asked about it Mattus said, "Häagen-Dazs doesn't mean anything. [But] it would attract attention, especially with those two little dots, the "oomlat" over the "a"!"

Later it was Steve Herrell and his Jewish wife who opened Steve's Ice Cream in a renovated dry cleaner's near Boston.

In those days most ice cream shops sold only three flavors – chocolate, vanilla and strawberry. Steve added mix-ins like M&M's, peanut butter and Heath Bars and business was booming – so much so that two nice Jewish boys, good friends, Ben Cohen and Jerry Greenfield, stopped by to watch Steve make his ice cream creations. They were impressed – so much so that in 1978 in Burlington, Vermont Ben and Jerry's was born.

So on a sweltering hot day when ice cream hits the spot, we can thank Ruben and Steve, Ben and Jerry – a fabulous foursome that represent ice cream's Jewish connection. Enjoy!

Gleanings and Meanings:

1. Reuben Mattus is an example of a determined and entrepreneurial Jewish immigrant. Among your friends, family and relatives, did you have anyone like Reuben Mattus? If so, share your story with us.

2. What is your opinion on Mattus' choice of a Danish name for his company?

Betty Boop's Jewish Roots

Today when grandparents share a video moment with grandchildren, it's likely that the image on the screen is the highly popular "Sponge Bob Square Pants." The show chronicles the adventures of Sponge Bob and his friends in the fantasy underwater city and is the highest rated series ever to air on Nickelodeon. But almost 90 years ago another animated character captured the hearts of the American public and today she enjoys a revival among cartoon enthusiasts. Who is she? She is the indomitable Betty Boop.

Betty's legacy dates to 1930 and her origins are steeped in diversity. Her voice derived from the African-American jazz singer, Esther Jones who performed as "Baby Esther" at Harlem's Cotton Club.

Betty's coquettish face is said to be patterned after the actress Clara Bow's iconic pout, while Betty's spirit was reminiscent of the aunt of Betty's creator, Max Fleischer. Max recalled that his aunt, Tantele Betta Boopinsky who, in Fleischer family lore, was remembered as "a feisty, go your own way kinda girl."

According to grandson Mark Fleischer, Betty Boop was the creation of a talented young man named Max Fleischer. He notes that Zayde Max was born into a Jewish family in Krakow, Poland, the second of six children and the son of an immigrant tailor who settled in Brownsville that, back in the day, was the poorest Jewish neighborhood in Brooklyn. Times were hard and when Max's father lost his business, daily life went from bad to worse.

But Max persevered, first doing odd jobs, then earning his degree in Commercial Art at Cooper Union College. Max married his night school sweetheart, Essie Goldstein and together they went west to California where Max became a cartoon creator and master animator.

And that's where Betty Boop was born. She first appeared in a famous cartoon, "Minnie the Moocher," where her character took an important turn. Her parents appeared on the scene and story after story focused on Betty's independence and how Betty was determined to rise up from the Lower East Side tenements and make it on her own.

The cartoon was revolutionary for two reasons: Betty was one of the first female characters with enough chutzpah to go her own way and even more amazing, Betty Boop was recognizably Jewish! In fact early cartoons featured Betty's mom and dad, speaking to daughter Betty ... in Yiddish!

In the very first episode, Betty's dad's yarmulke bounced on his head as he scolded her, prompting Betty to run away. Stifled by her overbearing immigrant parents, Betty was brazen and sultry, and eager to take this new world by storm even though she struggled with the fear of the unknown.

Ultimately Hollywood censors deleted Betty from movie theatre fare, (her skirt was too short and she sported a lacy garter!) but even though she was toned down, her sassy independence attracted a cult following that sociologists believed inspired many Jewish immigrants - especially those who were young and full of adventure.

Thanks to Max, Betty made so many of our *meshpucha* smile and laugh both at life and at ourselves, at a time when many immigrants and their children found themselves mystified by the new world around them. Betty's message was a timely one and one that resonates today. A new animated series, one that grandparents and grandchildren can share together, will air this year where Betty is revived as a modern young woman who dreams of becoming a superstar.

So we say *Mazel Tov* to Max Fleischer and his animated progeny, Betty Boop. As the Talmud explains, smiles are an even higher form of charity than giving money because the smile will enhance the recipient's well-being on every level of body and soul.

In Betty Boop's history and now revival we have another opportunity to keep a light hearted spirit alive in our hearts. Thank you, Betty Boop, for keeping an important Jewish tradition alive. Thank you for continuing to make us smile.

Gleanings and Meanings:

1. What do you feel made Betty Boop so popular over the years?

2. Do you see a relationship between Betty and her immigrant parents and the popular television shows broadcast today that feature Jewish families and Jewish themes?

3. How did Max Fleischer's immigrant background play a part in the creation of Betty Boop?

Meow-zel Tov!" Cats and Jews – a Lifelong Relationship

"She's my reason to get up early every morning," says Elaine B, assisted living resident whose morning habit could be motivated by her dedication to an aging relative or friend – certainly worthwhile endeavors – but for Elaine that's not the case.

"Sugar needs me," says Elaine, referring to her long hair, fluffy white cat. Elaine, the Jewish cat lover, is not alone. In fact there seems to be a strong connection between cats and Jewish tradition, and who knew? Having a *"chatul"* (The Hebrew word for cat) could be an innately Jewish thing to do.

In her article about Jews and cats, Shira Cohen-Regev tells us that since their domestication in ancient Egypt 3,600 years ago, cats and Jewish tradition have shared a common bond. In fact Cohen-Regev tells us that cats are mentioned fondly in the Talmud.

Our rabbinic sages, including the great commentator Rashi, note that cats are an example of modesty given their grooming rituals and use of the litter box and indeed the Talmud states, "If the Torah wasn't given, we would have learned modesty from the cat."

In his blog on the Jewish View of Cats, author Yonassan Gershom writes that many cultures have superstitions about cats, such as, "If a black cat crosses your path, it brings bad luck." Not so for us Jews, especially since our religion specifically bans a belief in omens (Leviticus 19:26). Instead Blogger Gershom recalls what Jewish comedian Groucho Marx once said, "If a black cat crosses your path, it means the animal is going somewhere."

Gershom continues that during the Middle Ages, when some Christians believed that cats were related to witchcraft, Jews saw cats differently. Possibly because cats were part of the culture of ancient Egypt and thus were familiar to Jews, this feline prejudice didn't exist. However for many European Christians it was a different story. Gershom writes, "So, in contrast to medieval Christians who were killing cats as demons, Jews kept them around to hunt rodents and protect the holy books from mice. In fact it was common to have a *"shul katze"* (synagogue cat) to protect the congregation's library.

When the Black Plague devastated Europe, sadly it was the Christian communities who suffered most. Why? Those "Jewish" cats that solved the mice problem also controlled the proliferation of the rat population, and thus European Jews were not as hard hit by the Plague.

So, nu, what is it about cats that lends itself to Jewish tradition? In an ancient Jewish text, *Perek Shirah* ("The Song of the Universe,") we find one answer. In these writings we are told that everything in creation sings a song to God. In fact it is the cat who sings, "I pursued my foes and overtook them, and did not return until they were destroyed." (Psalm 18:38.) This, Gershom says is "a pretty good description of a stalking cat!"

Back to Elaine who, when she emphasizes that Sugar plays an important part in her life, is right in line with current research on the relationship between pets and overall health.

As more and more elderly people live alone, having a pet can make an important difference in the daily life of an aging person. For Elaine, her cat Sugar gives her a reason to rise early since she must start her day by tending to her pet.

When Elaine says, "Sugar needs me," she echoes what gerontologists have determined as crucial to healthy aging – that is, having something to care for breaks isolation and increases an elderly person's interest in life.

Judith Siegel, Professor of Public Health at the UC Los Angeles tells us that elderly people who own pets also visit the doctor less frequently than those who are without animal companions. The thinking here is that possibly animals mitigate loneliness.

In a US New and World Report "In the Presence of Animals" (1992) Sarah Burke found that in a review of 25 studies on the effects of pets on elderly people in nursing homes, "Residents exposed to pets consistently smiled more and became measurably more alert than those who did not encounter animals."

Other prominent researchers concur that "animal companionship can dramatically improve the quality of life and may even have a positive impact on longevity."

But it is Elaine B, elderly herself, who sums up in plain language what all the studies seem to have determined. "I'm almost 90 and my Sugar will be 17 in September. What can I tell you? I do for her and she does for me!" – a sentiment that deserves a hearty Meow-zel Tov to Sugar and Elaine and their Jewish cat connection!

Gleanings and Meanings:

1. So what is it with Jews and cats? Do you agree that there is a special relationship?

2. Historically cats have been persecuted and maligned. Is there a connection between ancient society's beliefs about cats and its misconceptions about Jews? Why or why not?

3. Psychologists agree that having a pet contributes to the longevity of elderly men and women. Do you agree or disagree? Why or why not?

The Yarmulke Game

"Jill and Josh – June 21, 1978" "Chloe's Bat Mitzvah 2007" "Mazel Tov Sam and Zach 2016"

"I just don't know what to do with these," said Charna as she lifted a handful of commemorative yarmulkes from a bulging dresser drawer. "I've hung on to them for years," she said, recalling the simchas she's shared with family and friends. "I just can't let them go."

Charna is not alone. For many bubbys and zaydes the tradition of the personalized *kippah* (the Hebrew word for "yarmulke") has held a place of honor in the treasure trove of memories that Jewish families hold dear. But what to do with a drawer full of Jewish head coverings? That was Charna's question. Thankfully her good friend and creative bubby Shirley, had the answer.

"I was digging through my yarmulke drawer," said Shirley, "and it came to me. I could use all these yarmulkes to make a game for my grandchildren and great grands." And that's just what Shirley did. One rainy afternoon when two of her nine great grandchildren were visiting, Shirley pulled out the drawer and dumped about two dozen yarmulkes on the kitchen table.

"You kids can each pick a yarmulke," Shirley directed, as the children, ages seven and nine, plowed through the pile, selecting a color or style that appealed them. "Now," Shirley said, "Let's read what's inside." Taking turns the children read "David's Bar Mitzvah, November 10, 1988," and "Mazel Tov Jeffrey and Kim, July 4, 2011."

Now it was Shirley's turn. "Let me tell you about David's Bar Mitzvah," she said. "It was twenty-nine years ago, when David was 13 years old. How old is David now?" she asked? Shirley's great grandson quickly calculated that David of yarmulke fame now would be forty-two years old.

At this juncture Shirley, who shared that "David" is her nephew, offered a bit more information about him. "David lives in Arizona," she explained and asked, "Now you tell me, what do you think David is like?" And with yarmulke in hand, "David" came to life as the children speculated about living in Arizona, how hot and dry it must be, and what David might be doing for work and for recreation.

"Put David's yarmulke on your head," Shirley instructed her great grandson. "Now you're David and you're all grown up. Tell us about yourself." As the youngster began to weave a fantastic story about David as a superhero, Bubby Shirley phoned the real David and had him listen in.

"The kids love my yarmulke game," Shirley says. "They can create fantastic stories based on the tiny bit of information printed inside the kippah. Their imaginations run wild and we have a lot of fun."

When Shirley shared the Yarmulke Game with her mahjong club, the ladies were intrigued and several gave it a try. Shirley recalls, "One of the girls even videoed her five year old great granddaughter telling an incredible story about a magic yarmulke that when the bride put it on her head, she could fly. The bride in the story was my friend's great niece. She was tickled to see the video of this little one wearing the wedding yarmulke and flapping her arms like wings!"

Could it be that a Jewish item, something that among the many Jewish artifacts we've collected over the years – an item that might be thought of as less than ritually significant - could a little yarmulke really play an important part in sharing Yiddishkeit with the next generation?

In the words of Cantor Lorel Zar-Kessler, "We keep the memory alive by passing on the rituals we have received." Shirley would agree, not only with the cantor but with a *midrash* that states, "Looking leads to remembering and remembering leads to doing."

As Shirley looked into the yarmulke drawer, the midrash came alive. Precious memories returned – memories that can be shared creatively with future generations – all thanks to Shirley's taking an action by inventing the Yarmulke Game.

Gleanings and Meanings:

1. Do you have a drawer filled with yarmulkes? If so, do you look at them from time to time? Do they bring back memories?

2. What is your opinion of Shirley's Yarmulke Game? Do you think it will have a positive effect on the grandchildren? Why or why not?

3. As we downsize, what is the best way to keep or give away Jewish ritual items and gifts?

"Is It Me or Are Restaurants Just Too Loud?"

"No I don't want to go there. And not there either! How about we forget the restaurant and just eat at home!" Elaine just looked at her husband and shook her head. "Lenny, what's wrong. Eating out was something we always enjoyed, Now I need a crowbar to get you to go to a restaurant."

Lenny paced around the living room and finally spoke up. "Elaine," he said. "It's the noise. It seems that nowadays every restaurant is so loud. And it's not music. It's clanking and banging and voices that carry. We sit at a little table, right across from each other and we can't even hear our own conversation. Eating out isn't for us old folks. Restaurants today are for a younger crowd."

Lenny's lament isn't limited to the older generation. And the noisy restaurant complaint doesn't apply only to hearing aid users who have difficulty adjusting the mechanism to accommodate ambient noise. No, according to a lengthy piece in the November 27, 2018 edition of The Atlantic, ("How Restaurants Got So Loud,") journalist Kate Wagner reports that the noise level in American restaurants is appreciably higher – to the detriment of patrons and staff alike.

Armed with a calibrated decibel meter, Wagner tested the noise level in a variety of different restaurants, from coffee shops to fine dining, and what she found corroborates the complaint voiced by many diners.

Restaurants are just too loud – so loud in fact that conversations are impossible and a migraine should be a menu item. Wagner says, "Noise levels become harmful to human hearing above 85 decibels, and she reports that restaurants from Baltimore to New York City were often louder than this 85 decibel safety level, Wagner found decibel levels hitting 86 at a brunch in a food court and she recorded 90 decibels at a pub during a Friday afternoon happy hour.

So what accounts for the change from quiet to noisy that characterizes so many restaurants? Wagner (whose resume includes architecture and design experience) explains that the cultural shift from formal to casual dining is to blame.

As recently as thirty years ago dining was more elegant; soft music played in dining rooms where lush carpeting, brocade draperies and upholstered chairs were not only elegant but maybe more important, these design elements worked together to absorb sound.

Wagner writes that today "Restaurants are so loud because architects don't design them to be quiet. Much of this shift in design boils down to changing conceptions of what makes a space seem upscale or luxurious, as well as evolving trends in food service. Right now, high-end surfaces connote luxury, such as the slate and wood." Wagner writes that in addition many upscale eateries feature a preponderance of stainless steel, exposed ceilings and kitchens open to the dining room where patrons can watch their food as it is prepared.

Wagner goes on to say that "These design features are a feast for the eyes, but a nightmare for the ears," and she reminds us that the absence of soft fabrics and high ceilings mean that nothing is absorbing the sound. As Wagner puts it, "a room full of hard surfaces serves as a big sonic mirror, reflecting sound around the room. The result is a loud space that renders speech unintelligible."

If the increase in restaurant decibel level is bad for one's hearing, the cultural effects are equally detrimental. According to Wagner, "Noise also degrades the thing that eating out is meant to enhance - culture: a shared social experience that rejuvenates, rather than harms, its participants."

Is it any wonder that Lenny and many others like him are so distressed. "I've been to Bar Mitzvah dinners and wedding receptions where I can't hear myself think," says Lenny who faults the venue, and not the music, for creating such a negative experience. "We're shouting across the table, just to have a conversation. It's so uncomfortable that I just don't want to go."

Lenny is not alone. Restaurant patrons are lodging more complaints and others, like Lenny, are staying home; so much so that businesses are noticing the downward trend. But getting back to what Lenny would call a more civilized dining experience is not happening to any great degree. Why? According to author and design expert Allison Perlman, loud restaurants bring in more profit.

In her book, Smart Casual: The Transformation of Gourmet Restaurant Style in America, Perlman goes on to say that it's cheaper and easier to construct a restaurant interior out of hard surfaces – they're easier to clean, repair and replace, while loud restaurants encourage the adrenalin rush that comes from eating quickly, drinking more alcohol and wolfing down desserts.

For us Jews, the Book of Proverbs provides a guideline for the enjoyment of a meal when we read about the eating habits of righteous persons versus those who are wicked. "The righteous eat to satisfy their souls, but the stomach of the wicked still wants." (13:25).

What could be more soul-satisfying than eating a meal in a calm and tranquil venue? Or as Allison Wagner concludes, "I'm not calling for the return of stuffy, socially stratified fine dining

…. Rather, I'd welcome a return of a more relaxed and serene dining experience, one in which I can hear my dinner companion, avoid drinking too much, and dodge a stress headache following an after-work drink." I believe that Lenny would agree.

Gleanings and Meanings:

1. Have you ever experienced restaurant noise as Lenny describes it? If so, what if any action did you take?

2. How comfortable are you to ask that a proprietor lower the volume of loud music or a loud television in a restaurant or other place of business? If you've done so what was the reaction?

PART IV:

RESILIENCE – CARING

"Abandon me not when I grow old." – Proverbs 71:9

The Talmud's Take on Aging Parents

When I was about ten years old I knew enough Italian from my immigrant parents to understand the particulars of a heated argument. That day my father, who was about 50 years old at the time, was having "words" with his father, my "Nonno," who, at nearly 80 years of age, had recently moved in to our house.

As is normal, there were tensions between father and son, two Alpha males who were now sharing limited space. As tempers flared, I distinctly heard the pounding of a fist on the table. It was my grandfather who, pounding for emphasis, said, "No matter what our differences are, you are not to raise your voice to me. I am your FATHER."

I was stunned. Suddenly my big, grown-up father was a little boy, and just like Dad had done to me, Dad was being chastised by his father!

I recall this incident, which to this day stands out clearly in my memory, as I consider the mitzvah that requires us to "Honor thy father and thy mother." As we grow older some of us, due to physical and mental conditions, become childlike once again. And as children of aging parents we can lose patience with a mother or father who is less flexible, more rigid or confused.

Honoring one's father and mother is a concept that crosses all religious and cultural barriers, so maybe it's not so unusual that when our Talmudic sages wanted to share an example of this important mitzvah, they selected a non-Jew as our guide.

Rabbi Sholom Klass (z"l) (Tales from the Midrash and Talmud, Jewish Press), shares an intriguing story. The main character is Dama ben Nesina, a gentile of noble birth, who was admired as a wise and thoughtful man.

On this particular day the elders of the city gathered for an important meeting and Dama was invited as counsel and advisor. When he arrived they immediately seated him at the head of the table and the discussion began.

Unknown to Dama however, his mother, who today we might describe as one who suffers from severe dementia, had followed him and had burst into the chamber room. Before the startled eyes of the people, she rushed at her son and began to beat and slap him. When she kicked Dama, one of her slippers flew off her foot and landed across the room. Calmly Dama retrieved the slipper and returned it to his mother.

Rabbi Klass writes that the noble Dama, showing no sign of mortification or embarrassment, never raised his hand against his mother. Instead he gently patted his mother's arm and in a calm and quiet voice said, "Mother, allow me to take you home."

When the rabbis heard of Dama's remarkable self-restraint and how, even in her demented condition, Dama honored his mother, they announced, "*If you wish to understand how far the mitzvah of honoring one's parents extends, come learn from Dama ben Nesina.*"

In a Shavuot sermon delivered more than a decade ago, Rabbi Shmuel Herzfeld brings one of our greatest sages, Maimonides, into the discussion about honoring one's parents. Herzfeld notes that Maimonides was a careful and frugal writer, measuring each and every word. So it is significant that when the great sage used the Hebrew word for honor, "*kabed*", he used it in tandem with a form of the same word, '*le-hakbid*", to burden. Might it be that Maimonides is trying to teach us that while the obligation to honor a parent is huge, it follows that parents have an obligation to help their children perform the mitzvah – in other words to unburden their children of non-essential kvetching and, especially as parents age, allow our children to focus on the tasks at hand.

Indeed Maimonides discusses a case where a parent becomes too much for an adult child to handle. When that happens the great sage says that, "The child should leave the area and pay others to honor the parents on his behalf."

It seems that Dama was sorely in need of Maimonides' sage advice. Back in biblical times there weren't "Visiting Angels," (at least not the "help at home" kind), or residential settings where someone like Dama's mother could get the expert help she obviously needed. Yet absent modern day aging services, it was Dama's demeanor that makes the point.

The mitzvah states, without reservation, "Honor thy father and thy mother." In fact the mitzvah does NOT say, "Honor thy father and mother if they treated you well," or "Honor thy mother and father if they don't complain too much," or "Honor thy mother and thy father if they don't scream, yell and embarrass you in public." Dama's mother was indeed a handful, but it is Dama's behavior that informs our tradition. Whether the elderly in our care are our aging parents or grandparents, whether we are the aging family member, whether we are the independent senior or the more dependent one, our Jewish traditions offer us guidance in how to approach, behave and relate to the complicated process of growing old.

Gleanings and Meanings:

1. People with dementia often can behave in unpredictable ways. Dama's mother's appearance at the council meeting is just such an example. Have you ever been in a situation similar to Dama's? If so, what happened and how did you handle it?

2. Have you experienced memory loss in a spouse, sibling or partner? What are the challenges you've faced?

3. Put yourself in Dama's shoes. How do you think he felt when he witnessed his mother's outburst? Is it possible that at times our feelings obscure a considered choice?

Elderly Isolation – It's Bad for Mom But Worse for Dad

"We're so worried about Dad." That's how Karen began her email to me. "He's so lonely and my brother and I don't know what to do."

Karen's father, Sid, lived alone in the condo he once shared with his beloved Jennie, who passed away nine years ago. Today he rarely leaves the house.

The same is true for Gerry, except that he doesn't live alone. Gerry has a small apartment in a Jewish retirement community where activities abound, but like Sid, Gerry stays primarily in his apartment and although he takes his meals in the dining room, he often requests a table for one so that he can eat by himself.

Isolation and its effect on elderly men and women is not a new phenomenon but as the population grows older, researchers are finding that more often it is elderly men, more so than elderly women, who suffer from an isolated and lonely life.

According to Jared Wadley whose University of Michigan study of elderly isolation found that "men were more likely than women to be socially isolated," daughter Karen's concerns for her father are well placed.

Blogger Sarah Stevenson writing for the senior referral service, "A Place for Mom," speaks to Gerry's situation when she found that whether living alone or in a senior living community, a critical factor is NOT how many others are in proximity, but how often seniors engage in social activities.

And dozens of studies devoted to the aging process concur that social isolation increases the health risks for seniors, in particular for isolated men. These risks include long term illness, bouts of depression, diminished cognition, high blood pressure and an early death.

So, nu? What to do? One group that calls themselves the ROMEO's, offers a unique solution. ROMEO stands for Retired Old Men Eating Out and, as their website states ROMEO is "a simple acronym which helps to tell a very big story."

Thanks to Tom Brokaw who many say coined the term in his 1998 book, The Greatest Generation, the ROMEO phenomenon boasts local chapters located in cities all over the country and gives its male members an opportunity to meet, greet, share a meal and make a friend.

ROMEO founders emphasize the importance of their groups and cite a recent study published by Brigham Young University that states that making and maintaining social relationships (like the ROMEO groups provide) increases an elderly man's chances of a longer life by a whopping 50 percent!

When I found a ROMEO club near to Sid's home, I called his daughter with the good news. Karen was happy to learn that a socialization experience designed specifically for men existed but she had her misgivings. "So, Rabbi," Karen said, "The ROMEO club sounds great but how do I get my dad to go?"

Good question and B'Lev Shalem, an Israel based organization that focuses on "Personalized Support for Aging Well," offers several solutions. B'Lev Shalem staff suggest that adult children talk to their parents about the importance of social interaction for their physical, cognitive and emotional health, then offer to help them find opportunities that are engaging and stimulating and encourage them to try it, at first, "just one time."

Since men can be especially reluctant to break the isolation cycle, B'Lev Shalem suggests that adult children ask a friend or relative to accompany dad on his first visit to a new venue, such as a ROMEO lunch spot, or ask a current ROMEO member to serve as Dad's host the first time around.

Writing for the website, My Jewish Learning, Rabbi Bradley Artson reminds us that when "Moses and his brother, Aaron, receive God's command to appear before Pharaoh to demand the freedom of the Jews, in what looks like an unnecessary digression

… the Torah records that Moses was 80 years old and big brother Aaron was 83."

Rabbi Artson cites the Talmud where we learn that a person who reaches 80 has reached the age of strength and explains that "(an adult) of 80 years is finally able to look at the human condition with compassion and some skepticism. At 80 years of age, we need no longer serve either passion or ambition." Or as a ROMEO member put it, "We can sit back, enjoy life, make new friends and have a nice lunch!"

Gleanings and Meanings:

1. The professionals quoted here feel that isolation for men is more problematic than it is for women? Do you agree or disagree?

2. Have you ever isolated yourself from friends and family? What help, if any, did you receive to break the cycle?

3. How difficult is it to establish a new pattern of behavior and is it more difficult to do so when we are older?

Drug Abuse and Older Adults – A Dangerous Combination

It was touch and go but Sam survived open heart surgery. Although he had just turned 83, Sam was recovering well and his sons, Jake and Zack, were grateful and relieved.

As they left the hospital Zack reminded Sam that they'd have to make a stop. "You only have enough pain pills for three days," Zack said. "We need to fill the prescription so you'll have pills for the next two weeks."

"No way," Sam bellowed. "I'm not taking that stuff. I know what happens. You want more and more. Listen, kids. If I'm hurting I'll take some aspirin. That way I won't get hooked and turn into a drug addict!"

Jake and Zack rolled their eyes, shook their heads, passed the pharmacy and made for home. But both of Sam's sons were confident that in time they could convince Dad to "take his medicine."

Not so many years ago Sam's reluctance to take prescription pain killers was seen as an overreaction. After all, drug addicts, according to the stereotype, were street people, ne'er-do-wells and criminals. Seniors who needed pain medication were in no danger of joining that group. Maybe so, but Sam's sentiment wasn't so far off.

According to Drs. Mehmet Oz and Mike Roizen, "The United States has 4.6% of the world's population, but consumes 80% of the world's opioids, (while) a recent study found 25% of older Americans who are prescribed Xanax or Valium to help them sleep or quell anxiety become hooked."

Oz and Roizen claim that these percentages translate into an even more shocking statistic; more than two million seniors are addicted to prescription drugs. Senior abuse of alcohol and prescription medications is one of the fastest growing health problems in the United States.

Add ethnic issues into the mix and professionals find that drug abuse among Jewish seniors is of particular concern. New York's Jewish Home reports that "There is a pervasive myth that addiction is not a Jewish issue ... The myth that Jews are somehow protected from addiction reinforces shame and isolation and can inhibit Jewish seniors from seeking needed help."

For this reason The Jewish Home in New York City sprang into action, creating the Geriatric Substance Abuse Recovery Program. Launched in 2017 it is the first nursing home based, in-patient substance abuse program in the United States. The goal of the program is a straightforward one; trained mental health professionals and addiction specialists work with clients "to ensure that Jewish individuals and their families who are impacted by addiction find support within the Jewish community and receive education and a safe space to receive support."

Recently similar programs have surfaced, each one emphasizing that, just as young children and adolescents have psychological needs specific to their age and stage, the same holds true for drug addicted seniors.

Writing in the Pacific Standard, journalist Chelsea Carmona highlights the dangers of drug abuse among the elderly and notes that apart from the NYC Jewish Home program, there are only two other in-house elderly addiction recovery programs (Florida and Mississippi) in the entire United States.

Which begs the question; what can be done? If our aging mother or father seems to be self-medicating with a strong opioid, or if an elderly person realizes that she/he is drug dependent, where can they turn for help?

Drs. Oz and Roizen suggest that a visit to a general physician is an important first step, but even more important, seniors and their family members should emphasize to their doctor that the problem is serious.

They should press for referrals to psychologists, addiction specialists and support groups that are designed especially for older adults and choose a program that offers psychological maintenance and relapse prevention. Above all, seniors should be honest about how addiction is affecting their lives.

Author Debra Jay discusses the doctor – elderly patient relationship in her book, "Aging and Addiction." She writes that that some physicians have internalized the myth that either old people do not have drug problems, or that when they do, it's just too late to address addiction in any meaningful way. Jay goes on to say that "Even if a doctor approaches the issue, the older adult may simply switch doctors or deny a problem exists." The author points out that "It is usually the adult children who decide to take action and help motivate an older parent to accept treatment, through either informal or formal intervention."

Family intervention is easier said than done, especially when an addicted parent's behavior is manipulative, erratic or abusive. Our Jewish traditions teach us to honor parents, but as one Aish Rabbi emphasized, "that does not require honoring the sickness in them."

Where substance abuse is concerned, the aging senior is suffering from a disease – often hidden and unacknowledged but if statistics are even moderately accurate, a serious disease that needs understanding, attention and prompt intervention.

Gleanings and Meanings:

1. Over the years the Jewish community has believed that, in general, Jews don't get drunk or have problems with alcohol. Current research debunks that myth. What do you think are the contributing factors that have supported this myth?

2. Regarding drug abuse among the elderly, some doctors believe that that for addicts of advanced age, treatment is not necessary. What is your opinion?

3. In your opinion, is drug abuse among elderly men and women an important issue to address? Why or why not?

Bullies in Senior Living Communities

"I haven't seen you in the dining room for ages," Selma said as she rushed to greet her neighbor, Betty who lived on the on the same floor in their senior living complex. Betty wrung her hands and said, "I've been eating in my room. It's easier that way."

Selma was confused by Betty's response until the day that Betty finally opened up to her friend. "I don't come to the dining room anymore," Betty said. "Too many residents are mean to me."

At Selma's urging, Betty spoke with the retirement home's staff social worker who encouraged Betty to tell her story which reads like a textbook case of something many believed happened only among kids on the playground – At 84 years old, Betty was a victim of bullying.

In recent years US and international government organizations have adopted a definition of bullying and initiated programs to prevent bullying behavior. In fact the United Nations Education, Scientific and Cultural Organization (UNESCO) has adopted a definition that includes all victims when they say *"A person is bullied when he or she is exposed, repeatedly and over time, to negative actions on the part of one or more other persons, and he or she has difficulty defending himself or herself."*

Dr. Dan Olweus, a psychologist and founding father of the field of bully/victim research is responsible for UNESCO's current working definition of bullying. Olweus amplifies the definition when he explains that bullying is an aggressive pattern of behavior that involves unwanted, negative actions that repeats over time and involves a balance of power or strength. Experts agree and note that bullying can happen to anyone at any age.

Just ask Associated Press (AP) reporter Matt Sedensky whose recent article, "Senior Centers Grapple with Bullying Issues," received national attention.

In the article Sedensky interviews Robin Bonifas, a social work professor and author of the book "Bullying among Older Adults: How to Recognize and Address an Unseen Epidemic." Dr. Bonifas sites research that suggests about 1 in 5 seniors encounter bullying and attributes bullying to "a reflection of issues unique to getting older. Because elderly see their independence and sense of control disappearing, for some, becoming a bully can feel like regaining some of that lost power."

Sedesky spoke to Pamela Countouris, a consultant whose Pittsburgh based program focuses on staff training to combat senior bullying. Countouris emphasizes that "most senior bullying isn't physical but rather involves name-calling, rumors and exclusion and that women constitute the bulk of the bullies."

Selma's friend, Betty found this to be the case. When Betty finally disclosed details of her experience she said, "It started in the dining room. I'd wait to find someone to sit with. Some of the ladies would glare at me and whisper. Even if they had an open seat, they didn't want me at their table. When I asked, one woman told me they didn't like my flamboyant clothes and my waist-length braid. Another lady said that I wasn't right for their group. Others whispered "Leftover Hippy" whenever I'd pass by. Then they spread this gossip around to others. Finally I felt unwelcome everywhere."

A Google search nets nearly 100 websites, blogs, articles and even YouTube testimonials describing bullying among the elderly and what staff at senior centers and residences can do about it. One senior community in California partnered with a local nonprofit Institute on Aging and together they developed an anti-bullying program designed for senior citizens in resident facilities.

Another community invited local rabbis, priests, ministers and chaplains to address bullying from a faith-based perspective. One chaplain cited Rabbi Elijah Dressler who writes, "From the perspective of Jewish ethics passivity in the face of wrongdoing is almost as bad as committing the wrong."

Jewish tradition emphasizes that beyond helping someone deal with a problem like bullying we are ethically bound to view another person's problem as if it were our own. Selma did just that for Betty. If we observe bullying among the seniors, we can do the same.

Gleanings and Meanings:

1. Were you or someone you know ever bullied as a child? What happened and how fresh are those memories?

2. What responsibilities do we as Jews have when we see someone bullying another?

3. What can be done to prevent bullying behavior from taking hold among adults and/or children?

When Parents Outlive Their Children – A Tragic New Dimension

When Bernie celebrated his ninety-seventh birthday he was surrounded by friends and family – all but one. Bernie's daughter, Marsha was unable to make the trip from Boston to her father's retirement home in Florida. Marsha had undergone debilitating rounds of chemotherapy and did not have the physical strength to make the trip. Three years later, at his 100th birthday party, Bernie remembered his beloved daughter who had passed away the month before.

Researchers, doctors, sociologists and psychologists have written extensively about the difficulties faced by parents when a young child dies. The effect on the family – parents, siblings and grandparents – can be devastating as mothers and fathers cope with the deep sense of loss felt when a parent buries a baby, a toddler or a teen. But as the population continues to age and as longevity becomes more the norm than the exception, more and more seniors are outliving their adult children.

Journalist Allison Gaudet Yarrow agrees. In an article that appeared in the Jewish Forward (August 2011), "May You Live Until 120: DNA Uncovers Secrets To Jewish Longevity," Yarrow points out that general life expectancy is on the rise and remarkably, Jews are living even longer than those among the general population.

Yarrow cites British data that indicate that "Jews live an average of five to six years longer than their gentile counterparts, and there may be nearly three times as many Jewish centenarians as in the general U.K. population."

For us Jews this means that the possibility of our "oldest of the old" outliving their adult children could become a reality for many families.

Along with Bernie, mentioned earlier, Ida B. also has had firsthand experience with outliving not only a child but all of her children. Ida says, "I'm 107 years old and I have no idea why I'm still here, especially since my three children have all passed on. My two sons died in their seventies and my daughter was 82 when she passed. All three were a big help to me. I am so sad and don't know what I'll do without them."

Ida's plight was front and center recently when the country shared its grief with Roberta McCain who, at 106, outlived her 81 year old son, Sen. John McCain. And although Allison Yarrow reminds us of our biblical ancestors when she notes, "According to Genesis, Noah's grandfather, Methuselah, lived the longest, at 969 years of age ... Abraham reportedly lived to 175; Moses to

120," many elderly Jews acknowledge that living to 120 like Moses brings on its own set of problems, especially if their adult children pre-decease them.

Dr. Winifred Rossi of the National Institute on Aging, reports that "(the) Ashkenazi Jewish population... tends to live longer," while Dr. Nir Barzilai, director of the Institute for Aging Research at the Albert Einstein College of Medicine, who has spent years studying Ashkenazi Jews who have lived into their 90s and beyond, reports that their "exceptional longevity" is substantiated by recent genetic findings.

As the population ages, what can be done for an elderly parent who has lost an adult child? In a study that appeared in the journal, "Death Studies" (2016), researchers addressed the crisis. In the article, "The suffering in silence of older parents whose child died of cancer: A qualitative study," the authors encourage gerontology professionals to become aware. They write that "When an adult dies, the social support system nearly automatically directs its care towards the bereaved nuclear family. Parental grief at old age is therefore often not recognized and/or acknowledged."

What can be done? Health care providers need to be aware of the silent grief of older parents and offer services, such as support groups specifically designed for parents who have lost an adult child. In a CBC interview, Canadian chaplain Betty Silva, whose adult daughter, Rosemary, died of colorectal cancer, describes the grieving process and agrees that support services must acknowledge the special dimension of grief and fear felt by aging parents. "Listen and be available," she says and make sure support services are in place to deal with elderly parents who now find themselves steeped in sadness and fear of facing a future alone.

Gleanings and Meanings:

1. Have you or someone you know experienced the death of an adult child? If so, what were some of the ways you were able to grieve the loss and move forward?

2. When an aging parent loses an adult son or daughter fear of loss of a caregiver and confidant can dominate. What is the best way to help a senior facing this loss?

3. Can our Jewish faith and traditions ease the loss of an adult child? If so, what can friends and family do to support the aging parent?

As Holocaust Survivors Age – Special Considerations

Sergio Della Pergola, child of the Holocaust, was born in Trieste, Italy in 1942. He survived to become the leading demographic authority in the study of the Jewish population worldwide. An international award winning scholar, Della Pergola studied the effect of the government initiated and sponsored factory killing of Jews under the Nazis and applied those statistics to modern day Jewish numbers.

Given that we know that there are approximately 15 million Jews worldwide and given that somewhere close to 6 million Jews were murdered by the Nazis, Della Pergola asked, "Where would be today if the Shoah hadn't happened?"

Through his extensive research and demographic knowledge, Della Pergola extrapolated a number that is both magnificent in its remembrance and horrifying in its grief. Had the Holocaust not happened, there would be 32 million Jews in the world today.

In a recent article (Times of Israel, Sept. 2018), Della Pergola's statistics were again front and center when he said that the world's Jewish population has been rising by about 100,000 per year, yet the 0.7 percent Jewish growth rate is significantly lower than the overall global population growth rate of 1.1 percent.

What does it mean when we hear numbers like these? I am reminded of what my father (z"l) said to me when I was just a little girl. "Remember," he said, "We adults lost our families and friends, but you children lost that and so much more. You lost the promise of meeting, knowing and learning from Jewish children who would have grown up to be your colleagues and your contemporaries, your spouses and your best friends. Our loss was great. Your loss is immeasurable."

My father was a trumpet player, not a scientist, but apparently he was right, because professionals confirm that today we feel the loss as never before. Couple Jewish population studies with the diminishing number of Holocaust survivors and the picture is even more troubling.

A recent article in YNET news describes the harsh reality. They write that as of January 2019 there are only 212,000 Israeli Holocaust survivors.

Additional statistics emphasize that the number of living survivors is dwindling and by 2025, just 102,000 will still be alive. Then, according to a report published by Holocaust Survivors' Rights Authority, when the year 2030 arrives, only a quarter of the current number of Holocaust survivors—some

53,000—will still be with us – but many will be immobile and possibly incapacitated, especially since all of them will be over 90 years old.

In these days when anti-semetic activity is on the rise, when the Jewish population is behind the growth curve and Holocaust survivors are becoming too fragile for public speaking, what can we do to promote Holocaust understanding? Here are several considerations:

• Do you have friends who have Holocaust experiences yet to be told? If they feel uncomfortable discussing what happened to them, emphasize that time is of the essence and that the more that eye witnesses are willing to share their stories, the greater the opportunity to combat anti-semetism and foster tolerance and understanding.

• Are you a child of Holocaust survivors? Do you have friends whose parents are survivors? Psychologists report that there are specific behaviors, emotions and reactions experienced by children whose parents survived the Shoah. These children, many of whom are now seniors themselves, have a unique story to tell and through them the long term effects of the Holocaust on Jewish families will not be denied.

• Are you a child survivor of the Holocaust? Did you and your parents escape Nazi persecution? Were you hidden? Did your parents make the ultimate sacrifice by sending you to safety via the Kinder Transport, or did they hide you with compassionate Christians? If so, you have a valuable experience to share. In recent years psychologists have written about the credibility of childhood impressions and have come to understand that even children as young as seven years of age have memories that should be acknowledged.

• If you were a child during the Holocaust and experienced family upheaval or loss, do not minimize your story. One child victim, Clara, who is now 89 years of age recalls, "Our family was forced to abandon our home and the textile business founded by my grandparents and leave Germany in a matter of hours." When asked why she was reluctant to share her story, Clara said, 'I wasn't in a camp. I'm not a real survivor."

Survivors like Clara will soon be the voice of Holocaust remembrance. It is important that they have the chance to tell their stories in an atmosphere that is welcoming and respectful. Survivor Magda Rosenberg, whose entire family was murdered in Auschwitz puts it well when she cautions, "We're dying out. It feels like in another 10 years there won't be a Holocaust survivor left." If indeed our numbers are diminishing and survivor status is changing, it is imperative that we broaden our definition of "Holocaust survivor" and, welcome those who have childhood stories to tell.

Gleanings and Meanings:

1. Do you know anyone who survived the Holocaust? Are they still living? If so, are they physically able to tell their story? Do you or your friend ever worry about the social consequences when our survivors are no longer with us?

2. Why is it important for our eye-witness survivors to share their experiences? In order to achieve the greatest social impact, with whom should they share their stories?

3. The current group of survivors are made up of children who were hidden or who escaped deportation. How important is it that these stories be told?

PART V:

RESILIENCE - COPING

"A righteous man falls down seven times and gets up." –
King Solomon, Proverbs, 24:16.

Thanks to the *TorahNator* Seniors Can Access Shabbat Services

"I'm calling it the TorahNator," said a smiling Dr. Sandy, a resident of an Assisted Living and Nursing Home facility. "The minute I saw it I knew it was something special."

And special it is. For the ten seasons that I have had the honor and privilege of serving an elderly Jewish population I've worked hard to create adaptive measures so that more of our fragile residents might participate more fully in the Kabbalat Shabbat and Shabbat Shacharit (morning) services.

Residents who use wheelchairs and walkers, residents who are a bit unsteady on their feet, residents who struggle with cognitive deficiencies - many of these residents regularly attend our specially designed services, chant and sing the prayers, make Kiddush and enjoy challah after a rousing "HaMotzi." Yet something was missing. That's where the *TorahNator* made all the difference.

The Torah reading is the heart of the Shabbat morning service where one of our residents serving as "Ba'al Kore," chants 5-10 verses. One Aliyah blessing sung by the entire congregation announces the reading and one group Aliyah makes the concluding blessing. But it's what happens prior to the reading that has made an enormous difference.

"I used to carry the Torah," said a wistful Sidney S., who recalled the days in his home synagogue when he hoisted a large Torah scroll on his shoulder and during the traditional "hakafah" processional ceremony, Sidney reverently and carefully carried the scroll to each congregant. "How I'd like to do that again." And so the TorahNator was born.

As I watched so many of our residents skillfully maneuver their walkers, it occurred to me that a walker could be retrofitted to carry the Torah scroll.

Walkers come in many shapes and sizes and today they sport a variety of accoutrements so it wasn't difficult for me to find a walker that had been replaced with a newer model.

With a local handyman as my guide, we removed the walker's seat and refitted it with a plywood base. After measuring the spindles of our Torah scroll, we drilled two holes into the plywood so that the Torah with its mantle covering would fit securely into the plywood base.

Another of our talented residents created a multi-colored velvet covering for the plywood so that the TorahNator would have the dignity it deserved.

With the Torah scroll in place in its TorahNator, a majority of our residents now participate in the hakafah by rolling the repurposed walker forward to bring the Torah scroll to each member of our elderly congregation.

In a sermon given by Rabbi Barry H. Block (1996), the rabbi offers an elegant explanation of the Torah procession; Rabbi Block says, *"The hakafah, then, imposes a double responsibility, because both rabbis and lay people are included. We rabbis must ...help our community to know the tradition that is ours to do. As we carry the scrolls into the congregation, we recommit ourselves to this task. You, our congregants, as you turn to kiss the Torah, brought close to you more often than ever before ... (can), receive the hakafah as a symbol that you share in the responsibility to study the Torah and to do the mitzvot."*

In Psalm 71 we read these words; "Even when I am old and gray, do not forsake me..." Thanks to the TorahNator residents can indeed break through physical isolation and share in the responsibility that Rabbi Block so eloquently describes.

As elderly men and women take their turn at placing their hands on the walker's handles, and then pushing the TorahNator forward, they bring the Torah scroll to their neighbors and friends. The TorahNator offers everyone, including fragile elderly men and women, the opportunity to reconnect with rituals and practices that were once an important part of their lives.

Gleanings and Meanings:

1. Elderly Jews who want to participate in Shabbat and holiday services often have strength and mobility issues that prohibit them from attending longer, more traditional worship services. In your opinion how much adjustment is necessary to accommodate older congregants? How much, if any, of the service should be changed?

2. What is the responsibility of the rabbi or service leader to adapt a Shabbat or festival service to meet the needs of the elders in the congregation?

"I'm Getting Help" - Elderly Jews and Psychotherapy

"Hilda, you look fabulous," Gemma remarked as Hilda, her oldest friend, made her way to the table in their favorite restaurant. "No kidding!" Polly agreed as she noticed the positive change in Hilda as well.

What accounted for Hilda's transformation, that's what her friends wanted to know and Hilda was keen to explain. "I'm getting help," she said. No, not help with shopping, cleaning or dressing – Hilda's help was psychotherapy. "I've been seeing a therapist," Hilda said, "and he's made a big difference." Polly and Gemma nodded in agreement as Hilda continued, "After Marvin died I fell into depression. Even after two years, I couldn't shake the sadness. So I got some help."

Hilda's experience with counseling is not unique. In fact in an article written by Tom Jacobs that appeared in Pacific Standard, (Why Jews Make Good Therapy Patients, April 2012), Jacobs describes a study conducted with elderly New Yorkers where researchers found that Jews are "more open to sharing their feelings and concerns and more confident in a therapist's ability to help," than members of any other ethnic group.

The study, published in the Journal of Religion and Health, notes that among ethnic and religious groups including African-Americans and Caucasian members of other religions, the researchers found that "when it comes to getting professional treatment for anxiety, depression or other mental health disorders, the biggest divide may not be between blacks and whites but between Jews and everyone else."

The researchers posit a theory that among other ethnic and religious groups, the social stigma associated with seeking counseling or psychotherapy historically has been great. In fact, researcher Elizabeth Midlarsky of Columbia University notes that among African-Americans many held negative attitudes toward seeking help for mental health difficulties, "while Americans from European Christian backgrounds regard therapy in similarly negative terms."

Midlarsky goes on to explain that the attitude of the "rugged individualist," that is, one "who is self-reliant, independent, autonomous and reluctant to appear helpless, weak and dependent on others ..., appears to stand in direct contrast to help-seeking for mental health concerns."

The study, which relied on in-home personal interviews with 307 New Yorkers between the ages of 64 and 98, half of whom were Jewish, emphasized findings that support our friend Hilda's perspective as well as the reactions of her girlfriends, Gemma and Polly.

The research team found that "Jewish participants were not likely to perceive themselves as responsible for the cause of their problems, but were significantly more likely to perceive themselves as responsible for solutions."

Why is this the case? Why do elderly Jews feel so positive about seeking help for psychological problems? Once again, the researchers determined that "The differences seem to be mainly a matter of societal norms. Jewish culture encourages introspection and self-knowledge and places a positive value on help-seeking behavior."

Tufts University psychiatrist Ronald Pies agrees. Pies pointed out strong similarities between Cognitive Behavioral Therapy (CBT) and ancient Jewish teachings. As Pies himself concludes, both rabbinical Judaism and Cognitive Behavioral Therapy share "the conviction that human beings can exercise their reason in the service of self-improvement, self-control, and self-discipline."

In an article that appeared in the online publication, JewishWomen.org, Sara Esther Crispe turns to Torah when she says, "The Torah has always advocated the idea of having someone to speak with. In fact Chassidic teaching stresses that each person needs to find him or herself a *mashpia*, basically a counselor, someone with whom you can speak and who can help give you guidance."

Crispe points out that "In Ethics of Our Fathers we read, "*Aseh lecha rav,*" make for yourself a teacher, "*uk'neh lecha chaver,*" and get yourself a friend."

For elderly Jews, like Hilda, Polly and Gemma, and for all of us, this means that we understand how important it is to have people in our lives, including mental health professionals, to whom we can turn for empathy, help and advice.

Gleanings and Meanings:

1. Among older generations the quest for psychological help has been seen by some as an example of emotional weakness. What can be done to combat this misconception?

2. Hilda openly admitted that she needed help to combat depression. Have you or a loved one suffered from depression and if so, were there any synagogue or general community services that were of particular help to you?

3. Are there any Jewish traditions, beliefs or ethics that facilitate reaching out for emotional support? Share your thoughts on how Judaism can be a helpful conduit.

The Spiritual Bucket List

Well I made it another New Year," Saul said. "But will we make it to the next one?" mused Ellie. Saul and Ellie sat at a table sipping coffee (decaf, of course!) thinking about the year that was and the year ahead. "Rosh HaShanah's come and gone and there are still things we want to do," Saul said, "but who knows how much time we've got left?"

Saul and Ellie may not have said it in so many words, but they are talking about a concept called "The Bucket List," first popularized by screenwriter Justin Zackham in the 2007 movie of the same name. In the film Jack Nicholson and Morgan Freeman portray characters, each dealing with a terminal cancer diagnosis, who decide to put their wish list into action by seeing and doing all the things they've only talked about but never got around to accomplishing.

Although the Bucket List idea now has its own website (Bucketlist.org) with more than 400 thousand participants and 4 million items on its "To Do" list, some historians believe that the term itself has to do with an ancient religious practice where a bucket of holy water was placed the foot of the bed where a deceased family member was laid out. When mourners came to visit the body, they would dip their hand into the bucket and sprinkle the departed with holy water.

Others believe that the term, "Bucket List", originated in the Middle Ages and derives from a grisly practice of placing a bucket under the feet of a condemned criminal who was about to be hanged – an act accomplished when the executioner "kicked the bucket."

Later the idiom was used generally as a slang term for death as in Joe 'kicked the bucket.'

Regardless of its historical context, Blogger K. Dean among others notes that "many people believe that creating a bucket list channels your energies into accomplishing goals rather than wasting the time we have on Earth on things that don't matter." If that's true, the advent of a new Jewish Year might be the perfect time to consider a Spiritual Bucket List.

Dr. Erica Brown thinks so. In 2016 she shared her ideas regarding a Spiritual Bucket List in a provocative article that appeared in the Jewish World Review.

In her piece Dr. Brown refers to the Book of Psalms (90:12) where we read, "So teach us to number our days that we may get a heart of wisdom." Dr. Brown goes on to explain that our TaNaK (Hebrew Bible) is filled with stories of death bed scenes and although our biblical heroes didn't know from the phrase, "bucket list," Dr. Brown explains that "they had a very deep understanding that the last words, blessings and demands one makes are listened to with a different kind of attention."

So to all of our Sauls and our Ellies who wonder if they will see another Yontiff, Dr. Brown encourages you to consider creating and then accomplishing your own Spiritual Bucket List. Some ideas include:

1. Make that donation that you've been meaning to do. Write the check and put it in the mail.

2. Volunteer in a school, daycare center, senior center or synagogue.

3. Read the weekly parsha and talk to a friend about it.

4. Clear up a misunderstanding.

5. Reconnect with a childhood friend.

6. Compliment someone on a job well done.

7. Open the jewelry box and select pieces to give to your grandchildren. Write a short note about the history of each piece.

8. Shred useless documents and recycle the scraps, knowing that when you pass on you've made the sorting process easier for your children.

9. Even if it's just for 5 minutes, get outside and enjoy a meditative moment surrounded by nature.

10. When you become annoyed or angry, apologize right away.

In the film, Morgan Freeman muses that "Forty-five years go by pretty fast." Jack Nicholson agrees when he says that "the years pass like smoke through a keyhole." They're gone before we even notice.

Creating and dedicating oneself to a personal Spiritual Bucket List offers us, in our later years, the tranquility of focusing on what is important and the comfort that comes with making things right.

Gleanings and Meanings:

1. Have you ever created a Bucket List or considered things to accomplish before you pass on?

2. Why might a Spiritual Bucket List be important to aging seniors?

3. What items in Dr. Brown's Spiritual Bucket List appeal to you? Which one or two might you try?

The Blessings of Hospice

"Hospice is suicide!" That's what Dad said anytime the subject of death came up, which happened quite a lot in those last few years, especially since so many of his dear friends had died. "I can't believe anyone would even think about it," Dad would say. "Going to a hospice is like signing your own death sentence!"

Clearly this was not a subject that Dad took lightly and although he had had very little personal experience with a hospice program, he thought he knew what it was. But Dad's perceptions were based on insufficient information, colored by the fear of the unknown.

Sadly our beloved Dad had a health condition that was progressive and soon the powerful medicines that he had taken for so many years were no longer effective. We learned that Dad's options were limited. One choice was nursing home care and aggressive treatment which might extend his life by a few months, but would not relieve the feeling Dad had described so graphically. He'd say, "I feel like I'm drowning. I hate the feeling and it scares me."

The second choice was a hospice program. I was elected to explain Dad's options to him. Although I was not averse to discussing anything related to death and dying, I was troubled by what Dad always said about hospice. I wasn't looking forward to this meeting.

"I have some bad news for you, Dad," I began. "It seems that your heart problem just isn't going to get any better." I explained about the aggressive treatment but Dad interrupted me in mid-sentence. "What are my options?"

"Here it comes," I thought and took a deep breath. The doctor says that you could go into hospice." I waited. I knew that even in his weakened condition Dad could still roar. So I waited to hear, "Hospice is suicide!" But the roar never came. Instead he said, "Tell me more."

I took his hand and told him that hospice was a pleasant place, that the staff was warm and caring and that their mission was to keep the patients comfortable and pain-free.

"Sounds good to me," Dad said, as he was about to drift off to sleep. I bent down to kiss him and told him that I was off to find a bite to eat. He looked up, smiled and pulled me closer. "Go to the north cafeteria," he whispered. "The coffee there is free."

A few days later, Dad was admitted to a hospice facility on Florida's east coast. It was beautiful, bright and cheerful, with rooms that opened on to lovely gardens and patios.

There were snacks available for family members who were encouraged to come often and stay as long as they liked. There were cots that could be placed beside the loved one's bed so that friends and family could spend the night. And they even had a parrot named "Elvis" who loved listening to all the different cell phone ring tones and melodies that everyone enjoyed without the usual hospital restrictions.

Yet more than the place, it was the people who made all the difference. Each hospice nurse was trained not only in medical procedures for alleviating pain, but in the equally important area of relationships. Staff and volunteers explained the process of dying to us in terms as beautiful and loving as any poem or song ever written.

The staff doctor and rabbi were available to us and pamphlets explained what needed to know. When things became difficult between family members, a staff member was ready to find a private space to mediate the problem. No one was ever too busy to give us a hug or hold our hands.

Most important of all, Dad relaxed. He smiled, talked, and when he could no longer speak, he listened with knowing eyes as we shared precious memories and told him that we loved him. His sons and his best friend were with him when he passed away.

Dying is never easy, not for the person experiencing the end of his life or for the family who will miss their loved one so much. Yet Jewish traditions teach us that death is a part of life. As natural as it is to be born, so is it natural for us to pass on. In fact a wise rabbi once said that "Passing away to the 'world to come' is God's opportunity denied to no one."

Our Jewish mystics, the Kabbalists, say that our loved ones are welcomed on the other side by family and friends who have gone before and that everyone meets and greets around the "reunion table." For me the pain of passing on is alleviated somewhat by this vivid and joyful image.

The wonderful people at hospice helped our family cope with the complex emotions that are a part of terminal illness. They renewed my faith in the goodness of people and in the presence of a loving and compassionate God. In the Torah we read that after his wrestling match with the angel, Jacob exclaimed that "God was in this place and I... I did not know." Like Jacob our family had an eye –opening experience. In the loving arms of hospice, we felt God's presence and God's grace.

Gleanings and Meanings:

1. In its early years hospice programs were met with fear and skepticism. What might have generated this negative impression and what do you see as the positive aspects of hospice care?

2. Have you or someone you know experienced hospice care for a loved one? IF so what was your impression of hospice care?

3. Jewish tradition states that it is a special blessing to share final moments with a loved one as they pass on. What are your feelings regarding remaining with someone as they pass?

When Times are Tough Is Laughter the Best Medicine?

About 25 years ago, in the mid to late 1990's, when personal communication via the internet was coming into its own, many seniors, like my friend's father, Sam, couldn't wait to power on. Mostly Sam talked with other seniors, retirees who shared holiday and birthday greetings and most of all, jokes.

I recall Sam's belly laugh each time his friend Murray sent him some off-beat or off-color joke and how Sam searched his memory to send back another funny story, aimed at besting Murry in the mirth factor. How these guys loved to laugh.

Sam wasn't a doctor and neither were any of his friends, but they didn't need to be. They knew something then that most doctors believe today; that indeed laughter is often the best medicine.

As far back as 15 years ago the prestigious journal, Psychology Today agreed. The publication featured an article by Hara Estroff Marano who reported that doctors had begun to tout the curative properties of laughter. Hara Marano wrote that "Laughter reduces pain, increases job performance, connects people emotionally, and improves the flow of oxygen to the heart and brain."

In recent years more experts have taken the time to examine the results of patient laughter and have come to agree that, "Laughter sets off a chain reaction throughout the body that promotes physical and psychological health. Regular and frequent guffawing can both prevent illness and help you get well." (Victoria Vogt www.sciencehowstuffworks.com)

Which brings me to Louis Feinberg, Lester Horowitz, and Moses Horowitz, nice Jewish boys from Brooklyn who were better known as Curly Larry and Mo, of the comedy team, "The Three Stooges. "

While critics sniffed that the trio was vulgar, lacked aesthetics, and brought conventional comedic style to a new low, the Stooges were responsible for some of the most iconic comedies ever made. Their humor was often raw and they were not great innovators, but as quick laugh practitioners, they placed second to none.

I confess. I never liked the Three Stooges but I liked how my father liked them. Dad was educated in Berlin, played classical trumpet and was a voracious reader in at least five languages. But when the Stooges came on television, he'd roar with laughter. Following Dad's debilitating heart attack, the Stooges continued their laugh therapy and although I have no scientific data to confirm it, I have always felt that Dad survived as long as he did thanks to Curly, Larry and Mo.

Recently medical professionals report and research confirms something that many doctors and nurses understood for years—that laughter affects a patient's immune system by increasing the production of antibodies. These antibodies form a firewall against an impressive group of diseases, including viruses and bacterial infections. Even more, a sustained belly laugh can stave off depression and anxiety, prevent disease and help you get well.

Thousands of years ago our Jewish traditions understood how important laughter is to our mental and physical health. In Proverbs we read that "A merry heart does good like a medicine," while the Psalmist recalls that "God has a smile on his face," and that "Our mouth was filled with laughter, and our tongue with shouts of joy."

But if my Dad were here he would agree with his personal comedic sage. That would be Curly who would certainly punctuate the discussion with a hearty "Nyuk-Nyuk-Nyuk!".

Gleanings and Meanings:

1. Television shows? Cartoons? Comedians? Movies? Jokes? Funny Personal Stories? What makes you laugh?

2. Can you share a funny moment when you laughed out loud?

3. If humor ameliorates a sad or difficult situation, how does humor actually work to change our outlook or mood?

PART VI:

RESILIENCE: MOVING FORWARD

*"He who learns from the old, to what can he be compared?
To one who eats ripe grapes and drinks aged wine."* – *Pirkei Avot*
4:20

Seniors in the Workforce - "Should I Go Back to Work?"

Sheila's face said it all. In recent months Dina noted that her best friend rarely smiled and seemed out of sorts, sad and drained of enthusiasm. Finally Dina broached the subject; "Sheila, what's wrong. In all our years I've never seen you like this? "

That's when Sheila opened up. "I used to do so much," she said. "I loved my job and really never wanted to retire. But I'm coming up to 74 on my next birthday. I want to be useful again but who's going to hire and old lady like me?"

Sheila's dilemma is a common one but also one that has not gone unnoticed – at least not by the Bureau of Labor Statistics that began to examine an interesting trend.

In 2017, according to the Bureau's job report, 19 percent of seniors ages 70 to 74 were still working at least part-time. The agency also notes that seniors are working nearly 10 years beyond the traditional retirement age of 65 years old.

Danielle Kunkle Roberts is a member of the prestigious Forbes Financial Council and contributes regularly to the online publication, "Boomer Benefits." Roberts writes (November 23, 2018) that "back when Social Security and Medicare were created, 65 was the normal age at which people retired." Now, more than a half century later, things are very different. Roberts reports that "jobs for senior citizens are on the rise across America, and it's a really good thing."

In response to Sheila who asks, "Who's going to hire an old lady like me?" apparently there are dozens of companies that are looking for the skills, the temperament and, most of all, the work ethic that seniors bring to the workplace.

In her article "How Companies Are Making Room for Baby Boomers to Stay in the Workforce," Roberts offers specific examples of jobs for seniors and cites the CVS pharmacy company as one of the best. They're called the "CVS Snowbirds," and represent a unique program that has been a front runner in senior employment. The company provides flexible scheduling options "that encourage seniors to fill a variety of available jobs from cashiers to photo techs. The company feels that would-be retirees add value as they can directly relate and interact with the company's target market."

Other national companies have worked actively to retain and attract seniors to their employee pool. The Marriott Corporation created the "Flex Options" program specifically designed to help older Marriott team members transition from physically demanding jobs into other roles by offering on-the-job training that allows them to acquire new skills."

Seniors who worked as contractors or who have expertise in the trades are valuable resources to Home Depot whose program, "Senior Experts," employs a work force that taps into the decades of experience that "boots on the ground" seniors bring to the job.

As consultants, these seniors are contributing their building talents and time-tested ideas without engaging in the hard labor that once characterized their work day.

In our Jewish tradition we call it "*zaken*," the wisdom that comes with age, and thanks to medical advances and a general societal emphasis on wellness, seniors have longer life spans and in general are healthier than the elderly of generations past – a societal advancement that allows seniors to share their "zaken" with colleagues and co-workers.

Couple that with the fact that many jobs require less physical exertion, many seniors who return to the workforce, either full time or part time, find that it is easier to work well past retirement age.

What that means, Kunkle Roberts says, is that "for the first time in modern history, there are 5 generations of Americans working together, collaborating and coexisting in our workplaces."

Rabbi Dayle A. Friedman, who writes on the "Positive Aspects of Aging," for the Reconstructionist Jewish movement's innovative "Ritualwell" program, puts it best when she reminds us that *"The guidance of elders is seen as critical to the survival of the people of Israel: For one who takes advice from elders never stumbles."* (Exodus Rabbah 3:8).

Seniors have wisdom, experience and practical skills that are essential in today's world of work. US companies are becoming more and more aware of what seniors have to offer as they create opportunities that celebrate *"zaken,"* the wisdom that comes with age.

Gleanings and Meanings:

1. If you are a senior, what work did you do in the past? Are you working now?

2. What are some of the ways that younger bosses and co-workers react to older colleagues?

3. Many employers hire seniors because their work ethic is superb. What are the elements of a senior's work ethic that appeal to today's employers?

A European Wedding or an Island Bar Mitzvah – Tips for Seniors on the Destination Family Simcha

"Well I never thought I'd see the day," exclaimed Eva to her senior living buddy, Gladys. "When did this happen? When did you start using a cane?"

"That's 'canes' ….plural," Gladys' husband, Ken explained. "We bought two of them to take to Italy. Our grandson is getting married over there and we're going prepared!"

According to recent statistics regarding venues for destination weddings, Europe is one of the most popular choices and Italy tops the charts. At a whopping 78 percent of wedding destinations, FindYourItaly.com reports that "Bella Italia" is the European country most preferred with more than seven thousand destination weddings conducted there in 2017 alone.

The same holds true for Bar and Bat Mitzvah ceremonies. As more and more families examine alternatives to the "big bash" or "blow-out party," that, according to Rob Eshman, editor of Jewishjournal.com, can cost from $20,000 to $100, 000, more families are taking their show on the road.

Favored destinations include Europe, the Caribbean and of course, Israel, but no matter where in the world the ceremonies are held, grandparents hold a place of honor in these celebrations.

That's why Gladys and Ken, neither of whom are required to use a cane, chose to purchase a matched set, precisely for their European trip. In addition, this Bubby and Zayde duo put their *"kopfs"* together to devise a list of senior considerations when traveling abroad for a family simcha:

1. Have a frank talk with the wedding couple or the Bar/Bat Mitzvah family – Gladys and Ken were honored that their grandson invited them to offer a special wedding blessing, while other seniors *kvell* at being a part of the Bar or Bar Mitzvah service. But seniors report that prior to finalizing plans a frank talk with the family is essential, especially before the family selects a venue. Gladys and Ken emphasize that if you are frail or a bit un-steady, discuss your accessibility needs **before** the family makes a deposit on that spectacular but remote villa or hotel. Be proactive. Ken even asked to speak directly to the on-site event planner to discuss specific needs.

2. Ask the right questions. Does that ancient castle that presents so beautifully on the website have accessible bathroom facilities? Does the walled city where the villa is located prohibit auto traffic and if so, how much time is necessary to walk to the venue itself? Is there golf cart transportation for seniors and if so, how are those reservations made and guaranteed?

For example, the town of Ravello on the Amalfi Coast is accessible only on foot. A beautiful wedding villa is located at the end of long pedestrian passageway where the uneven pavement, dozens of steps and semi-steep grades present a real challenge for elderly guests.

Then there's the synagogue in Rhodes, Greece, built in 1577. It features a mosaic floor that, although breathtakingly beautiful, makes walking and even standing quite challenging, while the synagogue in St. Thomas (US Virgin Islands) is located atop a steep incline and boasts a sanctuary floor covered with sand. As Ken said, "These things are good to know ahead of time."

3. Photos, videos, Face Time or - "*Don't worry Bubby, we'll Face Time the ceremony.*" For seniors who are unable to travel, being present virtually, in real time, seems like an easily accomplished alternative, however it is important to determine in advance how this might happen.

Ken and Gladys found that some venues are so remote that limited band width prohibits a clear transmission, while some officiants discourage any cell phone use during the ceremony.

If a smart phone will transmit the ceremony, be sure to contact the officiating rabbi for her/his guidelines so that if real time technology is permitted, you can bring a stand or pedestal so that the phone can be positioned accurately for the duration of the ceremony.

In this way every guest can be emotionally and spiritually present during the ceremony. Better yet, consider hiring a professional photographer and videographer and organize a small reception at home so that those who could not attend can share in the joy of the occasion.

4. Do what Gladys and Ken did. Consider purchasing or renting an "all-terrain cane," (one of the most popular is the "Hurry Cane"). These super stable walking sticks feature rotating "feet" that adapt to grass, concrete and cobblestones and provide stability on ancient walkways and villa and castle grounds.

"American venues are mostly quit accessible but Europe is ancient and many buildings do not have hand rails, ramps or golf cart transportation," says Gladys, who reports that she and Ken practiced with their all-terrain canes for two weeks before departing the US for their family's Italian simcha. "We were ready," Gladys says. "We talked to the kids and asked the right questions."

Gladys and Ken got as much senior- specific information as they could. Ken says, 'We were like the Boy Scouts. We arrived prepared because no way were we going to miss my grandson breaking the glass!

Gleanings and Meanings:

1. As we age, accessibility issues take on increased importance when we plan family vacations and visits. The recent pandemic created even more challenges for the elderly traveler. Given these issues will you consider making a long distance or international trip?

2. When family members plan destination weddings or distance Bar or Bat Mitzvah celebrations, do you feel comfortable voicing your concerns? Would you feel included if your participation was virtual?

3. What advice would you give children or grandchildren who are considering a long distance celebration?

Aging Cancer Survivors Inspire Us

Thanks to statistics gathered and analyzed by the American Federation for Aging Research, as of January 1, 2019, nearly 2 million US adults ages 85 or older were counted as cancer survivors. In fact cancer researchers found that America's "oldest old" are the fastest growing group of cancer survivors, with nearly 4.7 million cancer survivors ages 85 and older expected by 2040.

In addition almost 1.5 million women over age 65 in the United States are breast cancer survivors, and over 820,000 of these women are age 75 or older.

When numbers become overwhelming it is helpful to focus on one survivor's story – a remarkable Jewish woman, Ruth Mosko Handler.

Each year in October Americans honor the memory of cancer victims and celebrate with cancer survivors. October is Breast Cancer Awareness Month and a great part of that awareness comes from none other than the *Barbie* doll.

Barbie was brought to life by a young Jewish woman, Ruth Mosko Handler. Ruth's parents were Polish Jewish immigrants. Her dad was a blacksmith who deserted from the Russian army and Ruthie's mom, who was illiterate, arrived in the US in the steerage section of a steamship.

A chemist by trade, Ruth worked in the plastics industry along with her husband, Elliot Handler. Elliot invented "Chatty Cathy," the first talking doll. Ruth invented *Barbie.*

Sparked by the feminist movement of the seventies, *Barbie* was criticized because some believed that the doll was damaging to a young girl's ambitions, and Ruth acknowledged that it was probably her impossible body that fueled the criticism.

But what was special about *Barbie* wasn't her dimensions. What made *Barbie* so unique was that she was the first doll that wasn't a baby doll but a doll that allowed a little girl, in addition to being a mother, to consider doing something else as well. Imaginations soared with *race car Barbie, doctor Barbie, police officer Barbie, hockey player Barbie, lawyer Barbie* and an all-time favorite, *astronaut Barbie, too.*

In 1970, when Ruthie was 54 years old, she was diagnosed with breast cancer and faced what back then was a woman's only option – a radical mastectomy. It was a time when few were open about a cancer diagnosis and support services were practically non-existent. So Ruthie, the chemist with expertise in plastics production and the woman who invented a doll with breasts, invented a prosthetic breast for herself.

Ruth Handler formed the Ruthton Corporation, the first company to design, manufacture and market the "Nearly Me" prosthetic breast. And all by herself, Ruthie trained a sales team of eight middle aged women, all of whom were breast cancer survivors themselves.

These women worked in department stores where they fitted women for prosthetic breasts and taught the existing sales staff to be sensitive and understanding to breast cancer survivors. Following years of national and international lecturing about early detection, including mammograms and self-examinations, Ruth Mosko Handler died in 2002 at 85 years of age.

As a breast cancer survivor myself, I salute and thank this brilliant Jewish inventor, mother and remarkable person, a true "tzadeket" – a righteous woman. May Ruth's memory be forever for a blessing and may she rest in peace in God's loving arms.

Gleanings and Meanings:

1. If you or a family member or friend is a survivor of cancer or another devastating illness, how important is it to talk about your experience?

2. Ruth's experience with breast cancer had life changing career implications. Have you ever had a negative experience with illness or loss that led you to a successful life change?

3. What is it about Jewish culture and character that motivates individuals like Ruth to accomplish so much?

Teaching Hebrew to Seniors – Materials, Methods and Positive Results

Not long ago five women were called to the Torah, each as a Bat Mitzvah. Not unusual except for the fact that the women on the *bimah* were all senior citizens, and, most significant of all, the students ranged in age from 82 through 97 years of age.

The women gathered once a week for one hour, to study the Hebrew language. They learned basic Hebrew and eventually each one was able to read three verses directly from the Torah scroll.

As their teacher, I was pleased and happy, as well as proud and astounded, all at the same time. In the process I learned that there are specific materials and techniques that can guarantee success when working with elderly students.

The Survey – Creating a Climate for Success

There are many factors that determine why a senior would consider studying Hebrew, as well as many reasons why she/he might feel reluctant to do so. I've learned not to assume but to help students identify their motivation as well as their fears.

So before designing the lessons, I asked students to respond to questions about their Personal Hebrew History, a survey I developed that consists of 15 statements. Students check any and all items that apply, such as:

"My parents sent me to Hebrew school but I don't remember much."

"I know the names of each Hebrew letter."

"I listened in when my brother studied with the rabbi. I learned the verses better than he did!"

From the specific information about what the students may have studied years ago, the survey questions also focused on the emotional in order to determine those issues that might become roadblocks to success.

Significantly, more than 90 percent of my senior students agreed with the following:

"I had a difficult time in Hebrew school. The teacher often embarrassed the students."

"I'm a bit nervous about class. I don't want to look bad in front of the group."

Past experience matters and negative experiences contribute to a fear of failure. Because long-term memories sharpen as we age, long ago embarrassments are so fresh that a senior may be reluctant to begin again. As a result, the first and most important challenge for the teacher is to acknowledge old wounds and then, to create a climate where students are free from competition and are rewarded for helping and supporting one another.

Materials that Work

The challenge for any teacher who works with seniors, is to select those materials that are basic yet not baby-*ish*.

Materials designed for children can evoke early memories of past failures. In addition, these materials can be less interesting to adult students.

The National Jewish Outreach Program (NJOP) offers a variety of materials that are not age-specific, but offer large print texts that are easy to use. The most effective lessons present Hebrew letters, not by their names, but by the sounds they make.

By Lesson Three in the NJOP program, students are reading and translating basic Hebrew words and phrases.

Sure Fire Methods

But even the best textbook cannot guarantee student success. The trick is to use the text in tandem with additional participatory activities - this combination is key to designing lessons that complement the special learning needs of senior students.

To organize the class sessions I found that I was most successful when I introduced three separate activities in a one-hour class and combined these activities with a short introductory review.

Class began with a short meditation, to clear our minds and focus on the positive. For example, *"Think of our last class. Remember something that you did well. A word you read well, a word you translated. Think of how you helped another student. Remind yourself that you can do it. You ARE doing it. You are learning Hebrew."*

Next, I ask the students to open their textbook to our previous lesson and take a moment to find sentences that they knew they could read smoothly. In this way class begins on a positive note and someone who has missed the previous class, can return to the last page studied and participate along with all the others.

Class includes text reading, presentation of new lessons and hands-on activities to reinforce reading and translating skill.

For example, many seniors have learned specific Hebrew phrases, such as the *"Sh'ma"*, by heart. Mastering Hebrew basics requires that students read each word. We accomplish this by placing each word on individual index cards and arranging the phrase in order, so that students can read, pronounce and translate the phrase word by word.

Positive Results

Often Hebrew study results in a Bar or Bat Mitzvah ceremony however that has not been my only goal. The result of the study program has been the delight of older adults who discover that the Hebrew language is not illusive, but vibrant, alive and accessible to everyone.

Resources:

The Hebrew Reading Crash Course – National Jewish Outreach Program, www.njop.org

The Hebrew Alphabet – A Mystical Journey, by Edward Hoffman, Chronicle Books, San Francisco, CA, 1998

The Personal Hebrew History Survey – Rabbi Barbara Aiello

Gleanings and Meanings:

1. What do you remember most about any childhood experience with the Hebrew language?

2. Do you think that the Jewish emphasis on Hebrew learning has changed over the years? If so, what changes have you seen and are these changes positive or negative in terms of Jewish continuity?

3. What is about the Hebrew language that makes it a special part of the Jewish experience?

Seniors Make Lifelong Learning a Literal Goal

For us Jews, learning knows no bounds; there is no end point where we no longer study and no age or era when we consider ourselves too old to learn. In fact, an important Jewish text, *Pirkei Avot* (Ethics of the Fathers) sums it up with these words; "*Do not say, "when I have time I will study," lest you not have time.*"

Texan Janet Schwartz Fein took these words to heart. After six years of study, Ms. Fein, at 84 years, and a former Jewish Federation professional, recently crossed the stage at the University of Texas at Dallas' commencement ceremony to receive her Bachelor's Degree in Sociology.

When asked about her accomplishment Ms. Fein acknowledged that she chose sociology as her major because it was "substantial," and went on to say, "I didn't thing that playing bingo was up to my speed!"

In a recent article penned by AP journalist Jamie Stengle the reporter notes that, according to the National Center for Education Statistics, "People 65 and older make up less than one percent of U.S. college students." Yet, although this percentage seems infinitesimal, in reality the numbers indicate that about 67,000 US senior citizens have enrolled in college or university programs.

Ms. Fein who revealed to reporter Stengle that she wanted her college degree "with all of my heart," explained that she participated in a Texas sponsored program that permitted seniors 65 and older to go to a Texas public university and take up to six credit hours of course work at no charge – a perk that nearly 2,000 Texans took advantage of last year.

And it's not only in Texas where seniors are having an impact on higher education. Thanks to Bernard Osher, son of a Jewish family that immigrated to Biddeford, Maine, the foundation he established is helping senior students who share Janet Fein's motivation to realize their dream of marching in cap and gown.

A successful businessman and entrepreneur, Osher owned and operated a large eclectic hardware store but is best remembered for his venture in Old Orchard Beach where he established Palace Playland, a famous summer amusement park.

But it wasn't until 1977 when Osher realized his dream which resulted in his establishment of the Bernard Osher Foundation – an educational philanthropy that has funded over 120 Lifelong Learning Institutes at universities and colleges throughout the United States.

Known as the "quiet philanthropist," Bernard Osher was determined to create scholarship opportunities for reentry students and "seasoned adults" who want to enlarge upon or continue their educational pursuits.

Thanks to Guinness World Records we know that in 2007 Nola Hill Ochs graduated from Fort Hays (KS) State University where she earned not only a Bachelor's but a Master's degree as well. Ms. Ochs, who passed away in 2016, received her Guinness Book honor because, at age 95, she was and is the oldest person in the world to receive a college degree.

It's clear that as Baby Boomers age, programs like those sponsored by the Osher Foundation that stand ready to help seniors connect or reconnect with higher education, will increase proportionately. And although neither Ms. Ochs nor Ms. Fein could be included in the Boomer generation, their initiation as senior citizens into college life exemplifies an important cultural change.

As Jamie Stengle reports, when Ms. Fein's physical condition prohibited her from driving, she kept on studying for her degree. When she began using a walker, she kept on studying. When schlepping an oxygen tank was added to her daily routine, she kept on studying and when her knees gave out and she moved into a senior living residence, she never stopped. Instead she enrolled in online classes so that she could remain on track to receive her degree.

In the spirit of our Jewish tradition of educational pursuit, Ms. Fein's college advisor lauds Janet Fein as an inspiration, especially to elderly students, and emphasizes that in the midst of challenges Ms. Fein did not give up. "She just kept plugging along

Gleanings and Meanings:

1. Do you think internet learning and virtual classrooms will help or hinder seniors who want to enroll In college or university programs?

2. If you could begin a program of study today, what topic would you study? What degree would you pursue?

3. Regarding life long learning, many seniors say "It's never too late?" How do you feel about that? Can we learn and grow in a structured environment even when we are quite old?

"Buy a Trombone"

For Harriet K. it's the piano. For Milton S. it can be either clarinet or the sax. For me, it's always been the trumpet.

As I watched Harriet's fingers fly over the keys as she sang the old time tunes and then, during a break in the sing-along, as I listened to Milton jamming on the sax, it occurred to me that I could add my trumpet to the weekly music mix in the Jewish retirement home where I served as resident rabbi.

Several weeks went by and work obligations demanded most of my time, but finally I headed up to my storage locker to find my trumpet – the very same one my father cherished and the one he played just days before he passed on. I've kept Dad's trumpet with me, playing only occasionally but I was determined that one day I would make sounds worthy of any one of the brass musicians that are part of Bruce Springsteen's E Street Horns.

"Owwww! That hurts!"

Rabbi decorum aside, when the doc's assistant ever so gently pulled on the middle finger of my right hand, trying to straighten the sticking joint, I let out a very unspiritual yelp.

Later the doctor gave me the news. "It's a condition called 'trigger finger,' and you've got it in both hands. It comes from doing repetitive motions." He went on to explain that "trigger finger" was an age-related condition and was a common ailment among musicians, especially trumpet players.

"So that's it," I said to my 70 plus year old self, "Just when I was going to join our seniors' music mash up, I won't be able to play in Milton's band."

In her book, Jewish Visions for Aging, Rabbi Dayle A. Friedman writes, "*The aging process challenges a person's sense of who she is, who she has been and what she will yet be. The accumulation of losses, the "little deaths" of the aging process moves us to redefine ourselves.*"

Faced with that redefinition, it is apparent that as we age we have two choices. While we adapt to each loss of motor dexterity or general physical ability, we can approach these changes as either victims or survivors.

The "little death" brought about by "trigger finger," offered me that same challenge. But first I had to tell Milton that I wasn't able to play trumpet in his pickup band.

It is Rabbi Friedman who emphasizes that "*In the Jewish tradition, first and foremost, old age is associated with wisdom.*"

Friedman writes that for us Jews the elderly are viewed as leaders that have good advice to share. In fact in the Torah we are told, *"Ask your father and he will tell you, ask your elders and they shall instruct you."*

I still hadn't spoken to Milton.

In the Book of Job it is Job himself who tells us that *"For wisdom is with the old, and understanding with length of days."* Taking those words to heart I approached my friend Milton, who at 90 plus, indeed fit the bill to "ask your elders."

As I poured out the long sad story of my physical disability in an endless stream of "Oh Poor Me," and how I thought "trigger finger" was a frivolous name for such a serious problem and how frustrated I was now that I had the time to play trumpet and couldn't. Blah Blah Blah…

Milton, my wise elder, a sturdy man steeped in a life of Jewish resilience and adaptation, stopped me in mid-lamentation and in a few words helped me move from victim to survivor. "Dahling," he said. "If it's music you want to make, stop *kvetching*. Buy a trombone."

Gleanings and Meanings:

1. The rabbi in our story mourned the loss of her ability to play trumpet. What changes and/or losses brought about by aging do you mourn?

2. Milton helped the rabbi see that she could move from Victim to Survivor – What does that mean?

ABOUT THE AUTHOR

Since 1999 Rabbi Barbara Aiello has served congregations in Bradenton and Sarasota, Florida, in Milan, Italy and in her ancestral home, the village of Serrastretta, in the Calabria region of southern Italy.

In Florida Rabbi Barbara served as resident rabbi at the Jewish retirement and elder care facility, Aviva, where she provided worship services, activities and lectures to meet the needs of the elderly Jewish community.

In Italy Rabbi Barbara is the spiritual leader for Ner Tamid del Sud, The Eternal Light of the South, the first active synagogue in Calabria in 500 years since Inquisition times. The synagogue is a recognized affiliate of the Reconstructionist Jewish movement and is "pluralistic," in that the approach is egalitarian. The hand of Jewish welcome is extended to Jews of all backgrounds – especially the "*b'nei anusim*," – those whose ancestors were forced into Christian conversion centuries ago.

Rabbi Barbara is the first non-orthodox and first and only woman rabbi in Italy.

As director of the Italian Jewish Cultural Center of Calabria, (IjCCC) Rabbi Barbara serves Italians along with Italian-

Americans and Italian-Canadians to help them discover and embrace their Jewish roots.

As a vice president of Kulanu, an international organization that supports isolated and emerging Jewish communities worldwide, Rabbi Barbara has lectured on the development of her synagogue and worked to bring attention to small and struggling congregations around the world.

Rabbi Barbara has been a featured speaker on the topic of Italian anusim and has traveled in the United States and in Europe as part of an educational program to bring the international anusim experience to the forefront of Jewish thought. Her recent book, "The Cat that Ate the Cannoli" highlights the rebirth of Judaism among the villagers who live in the isolated mountains of southern Italy.

For 17 years Rabbi Barbara was host of the Radio Rabbi program, broadcast live every Sunday morning on AM 930 The Answer in Sarasota, Florida, while in her previous life, before becoming a rabbi, she was founder and director of The Kids on the Block puppet program used around the world to teach children and adults to accept and appreciate difference and diversity.

Rabbi Barbara is a graduate of Indiana University of Pennsylvania where she received the Distinguished Alumni Award. She holds a MS from The George Washington University in Washington DC and following her participation in Hebrew Union College's Para Rabbinic Program, she received "smeicha" (rabbinic ordination) from The Rabbinical Seminary International and the Rabbinical Academy in New York City.

She has won several awards, among them Washingtonian of the Year, Parents Magazine's "Good Parent to Know," and the Surgeon General's Medallion for Excellence in Public Health from Dr. C. Everett Koop.

In 2015, Rabbi Barbara was the featured speaker at the National Press Club's "Newsmakers" program in Washington, DC. In addition she was invited to the United Nations headquarters in New York City as the guest of the Bahrain government where she was asked to present her international efforts on diversity, tolerance and religious pluralism.

Made in the USA
Coppell, TX
30 July 2020